DIABETIC DIET

COOKBOOK FOR BEGINNERS

100+ **Easy and Simple**	Low-Sugar, Low-Carb Recipes to Master Diabetes

Your Meal Plan and Shopping List for a
Healthy Lifestyle **After 50**

MIRA KENDELL

TABLE OF CONTENTS

CHAPTER 9: DINING OUT AND SOCIAL EVENTS 102

CHAPTER 10: MEAL PLANNING 103

HELLO AND WELCOME!

'm so glad you picked up this cookbook. Whether you have diabetes, are supporting someone with diabetes, or just want to eat healthier, you're in the right place. Managing diabetes can be tough, especially when choosing meals. But don't worry - I'm here to help you.

This cookbook simplifies life, improves flavors, and promotes wellness. You don't need to be a cooking expert to make these recipes. They are designed to be simple, so whether you're new to cooking or have been doing it for a while, you'll find easy and tasty dishes.

In this book, you'll find various recipes for every taste and occasion - from quick breakfast ideas to satisfying dinners, snacks to satisfy your cravings, and desserts that won't cause spikes in your blood sugar. I've also included essential tips and tricks to help you understand how food affects your body so you can make satisfying and healthy choices.

Remember, this isn't about strict diets or depriving yourself. It's about enjoying food that makes you feel good. So, get ready to explore new flavors, learn cooking techniques, and, most importantly, have fun in the kitchen!

Here's to an exciting journey of delicious discoveries and healthy eating. Let's start cooking!

With warmest wishes,
Mira Kendell

CHAPTER 1

INTRODUCTION

WHO IS THIS BOOK FOR?

You might be wondering if this cookbook fits you, so let me clarify that immediately. This book is for anyone who wants to control diabetes through delicious, easy-to-make meals—no matter where you are on your journey.

Are you newly diagnosed with diabetes?

This book is a great starting point. I know it can be overwhelming at first, but I've broken down everything you need to know. You'll find recipes that are easy to follow, even if you're new to cooking, and tips that will help you make healthier choices without feeling lost or stressed.

Have you been living with diabetes for a while?

If you've already been managing your diabetes, this book will offer you fresh ideas and new flavors to keep your meals exciting and enjoyable. You'll discover new recipes that fit into your routine and advice on tweaking your favorite dishes to make them more diabetes-friendly.

Are you cooking for someone with diabetes?

Maybe you're a family member or friend of someone with diabetes and want to help them eat well. This cookbook will give you the tools to prepare meals that everyone at the table will love while also supporting the health of your loved one. Plus, the recipes are designed to be accessible and approachable, so you don't need to be a pro in the kitchen.

Or are you just looking to eat healthier?

Even if you don't have diabetes, this book is for anyone who wants to enjoy balanced, nutritious meals that are low in sugar and packed with flavor. The recipes here are great for anyone who wants to take care of their health while still enjoying the food they eat.

No matter who you are or why you picked up this book, I'm here to guide you, inspire you, and make cooking more accessible and fun. Let's get cooking and enjoy the journey to better health together!

HOW TO USE THIS COOKBOOK

I'm so excited that you're ready to dive into this cookbook! Before you get started, I want to give you a quick guide on how to make the most of everything you'll find on these pages.

1 Start with the Basics

If you're new to diabetes or need a refresher, look at the introductory chapters first. These sections will help you understand how different foods affect your blood sugar and give you some handy tips for managing your diet. It's a great foundation to build on as you explore the recipes.

2 Browse the Recipes by Meal Type

The recipes in this book are organized by meal type — breakfast, lunch, dinner, snacks, desserts, and beverages—so you can easily find what you're in the mood for. Whether you need a quick breakfast idea or a hearty dinner, flip to the relevant section and start cooking!

3 Follow the Recipes Step-by-Step

Each recipe is designed to be simple, with step-by-step instructions that anyone can follow. You don't need fancy cooking skills to make these dishes — just a willingness to try new things and enjoy the process. I've also included nutritional information with each recipe, so you know what you eat.

4 Customize to Your Taste

Feel free to get creative and make these recipes your own! Don't be afraid to experiment if you have favorite herbs, spices, or ingredients. I've also included tips on adjusting the recipes to fit your needs, whether cooking for one, feeding a family, or preparing for a special occasion.

5 Learn and Grow

Throughout the book, you'll find helpful tips, cooking techniques, and little nuggets to help you build your confidence in the kitchen. The more you cook, the more comfortable you'll become, so don't be afraid to try new recipes and expand your skills.

6 Have fun!

Most importantly, have fun with this cookbook! Cooking is a great way to care for yourself and can be a gratifying and creative process. So, put on some music, grab your favorite apron, and enjoy the journey of making healthy, tasty meals that you'll love.

I hope this cookbook becomes your go-to resource, bringing daily joy and health to your kitchen.

CHAPTER 2

UNDERSTANDING DIABETES

OVERVIEW OF DIABETES: TYPES, CAUSES, AND SYMPTOMS

Let's take a moment to chat about diabetes. Understanding what it is and how it affects your body is an essential first step in managing it. Don't worry — I'll break it down in a way that's easy to understand.

What Is Diabetes?

Diabetes is a condition that affects how your body processes sugar (glucose), which is a significant source of energy for your cells. Usually, your body uses a hormone called insulin to help move glucose from your blood into your cells. But when you have diabetes, this process doesn't work as it should. As a result, sugar builds up in your bloodstream, leading to various health issues if not appropriately managed.

Types of Diabetes

There are a few different types of diabetes, and each works a little differently:

- **Type 1 Diabetes:** This type is less common and is usually diagnosed in children or young adults. With Type 1 diabetes, the body doesn't produce insulin at all because the immune system mistakenly attacks the cells in the pancreas that make it. People with Type 1 diabetes need to take insulin every day to manage their blood sugar levels.

- **Type 2 Diabetes:** This is the most common type and often develops in adults, although it's becoming more common in younger people too. In Type 2 diabetes, the body still makes insulin but doesn't use it effectively. This is called insulin resistance. Over time, the pancreas can't keep up with the demand for more insulin, and blood sugar levels rise.

- **Gestational Diabetes:** This type occurs during pregnancy in some women who didn't have diabetes before. It usually goes away after the baby is born but managing it during pregnancy is essential to keep both mom and baby healthy. Having gestational diabetes also increases the risk of developing Type 2 diabetes later.

What Causes Diabetes?

The causes of diabetes can vary depending on the type:

- **Type 1 Diabetes:** The exact cause isn't fully understood, but it's believed to involve genetic and environmental factors. It's not caused by diet or lifestyle.

- **Type 2 Diabetes:** This type is often linked to lifestyle factors, such as being overweight, having a poor diet, and being inactive. However, genetics also play a role, so if it runs in your family, you might be at a higher risk.

- **Gestational Diabetes:** Hormonal changes during pregnancy can lead to this type, especially if you have risk factors like being overweight or having a family history of diabetes.

Common Symptoms of Diabetes

Knowing the symptoms of diabetes is critical to catching it early and managing it effectively. Here are some common signs to look out for:

- **Increased Thirst and Frequent Urination:** High blood sugar levels cause your kidneys to work harder to filter out the excess sugar, which can make you feel thirsty and lead to more trips to the bathroom.

- **Fatigue:** When your cells aren't getting enough glucose, you might feel more tired than usual.

- **Blurred Vision:** High blood sugar can cause your eyes to swell, leading to blurry vision.

- **Slow-Healing Wounds:** Cuts and bruises may take longer if your blood sugar is high.

- **Unexplained Weight Loss:** This is more common in Type 1 diabetes, where your body breaks down muscle and fat for energy because it can't get enough glucose.

- **Numbness or Tingling in Hands or Feet:** This is a sign of nerve damage, which can occur if high blood sugar is left untreated for too long.

If you're experiencing any of these symptoms or have concerns about diabetes, it's essential to talk to your healthcare provider. Early detection and management can make a big difference in your health.

Remember, understanding diabetes is the first step toward managing it, and you're already on the right path by learning more about it. With the proper knowledge and tools, like this cookbook, you can take control of your health and live a vibrant life.

THE IMPORTANCE OF DIET IN MANAGING DIABETES

What you eat plays a huge role in managing diabetes. Think of your diet as a powerful tool to help you keep your blood sugar levels in check and feel your best daily. Discuss why your food choices are essential and how they can make a big difference to your health.

Food is Fuel

Just like a car needs the right fuel to run smoothly, your body needs the right balance of foods to keep your blood sugar levels steady. Every time you eat, your body breaks down the food into glucose (sugar), entering your bloodstream. If you have diabetes, your body might struggle with processing that glucose effectively, so it's essential to choose foods that help keep your blood sugar in a healthy range.

Balancing Act

The key to managing diabetes through diet is balance. This means including a mix of different food groups in your meals—like lean proteins, healthy fats, and plenty of vegetables—while being mindful of carbohydrates, which significantly impact blood sugar. Carbs aren't bad, but it is crucial to choose the right ones and eat them in the right amounts. Whole grains, legumes, and non-starchy vegetables are great options that provide energy without causing big spikes in blood sugar.

Why It Matters

Keeping your blood sugar levels stable helps prevent complications from diabetes, like heart disease, nerve damage, and vision problems. However, the benefits of a balanced diet go beyond just managing diabetes. Eating well can help you maintain a healthy weight, boost energy levels, and improve overall well-being.

Small Changes, Big Impact

The good news is that you don't need to overhaul your entire diet overnight. Small, consistent changes can make a big difference. For example, swapping out sugary drinks for water or unsweetened tea, adding more veggies to your plate, or choosing whole grains over refined ones can all help you manage your diabetes more effectively.

Enjoying Your Food

Managing diabetes doesn't mean giving up the foods you love. It's all about finding healthier ways to enjoy them. This cookbook is packed with delicious recipes that are both diabetes-friendly and satisfying. You'll learn to make meals that nourish your body and taste great so that you can feel good about your eating.

Staying on Track

Your diet is just one piece of the puzzle, but it's a piece you have a lot of control over. By making thoughtful food choices, you're taking a big step toward managing your diabetes and leading a healthier life. Remember, you're not alone on this journey — this cookbook is here to support you with recipes, tips, and guidance at every step.

COMMON MISCONCEPTIONS ABOUT DIABETES AND FOOD

When it comes to diabetes and food, there's a lot of information out there — some of it helpful, and some of it, well, not so much. It's easy to get confused by all the different advice, especially regarding what you should or shouldn't eat. Let's clear up some of the most common misconceptions so you can feel more confident about your food choices.

Misconception #1: "You Have to Give Up All Sugar"

One of the biggest myths about diabetes is that you can never have sugar again. The truth is, you don't have to cut out sugar entirely. The key is moderation. It's all about balancing your meals and watching your portion sizes. You can still enjoy a sweet treat now and then — make sure it fits into your overall plan for the day. And, of course, choosing natural sugars from fruits is always a better option than processed sweets.

Misconception #2: "Carbs Are the Enemy"

Carbohydrates often get a bad rap for diabetes, but they're not the enemy. Your body needs carbs for energy, so they should be a part of your diet. The trick is to choose the right kinds of carbs—like whole grains, legumes, and vegetables — and pair them with protein and healthy fats to slow down the absorption of sugar into your bloodstream. This helps keep your blood sugar levels more stable.

Misconception #3: "Diabetes-Friendly Food Is Boring and Bland"

Some people think eating for diabetes means giving up flavor and excitement in your meals, but that's far from the truth! You can enjoy many delicious, vibrant foods that are satisfying and good for your blood sugar. This cookbook contains tasty recipes that prove you don't have to sacrifice flavor for health. From savory meals to sweet treats, there's plenty to enjoy.

Misconception #4: "You Can't Eat Fruit"

It's a common belief that people with diabetes should avoid fruit because of its natural sugars. While it's true that fruit contains sugar, it's also packed with fiber, vitamins, and antioxidants that are great for your health. The key is to choose whole fruits instead of fruit juices or dried fruits and to enjoy them in moderation. Pairing fruit with a source of protein, like nuts or yogurt, can also help manage your blood sugar.

Misconception #5: "You Have to Eat Special 'Diabetic' Foods"

There's no need to buy expensive "diabetic" foods or unique diet products. Many of these products can be highly processed and not as healthy as they seem. The best approach is to eat whole, natural foods rich in nutrients. Simple, homemade meals made with fresh ingredients are often the healthiest—and tastiest—options.

Misconception #6: "Only Overweight People Get Diabetes"

While it's true that being overweight is a risk factor for Type 2 diabetes, it's not the only cause. Diabetes can affect people of all shapes, sizes, and backgrounds. Factors like genetics, age, and lifestyle all play a role. So, it's crucial for everyone, regardless of weight, to be mindful of their diet and health.

Misconception #7: "Once You Have Diabetes, You Can't Eat Out"

Eating out with diabetes is possible — you just need to make smart choices. Many restaurants offer healthy options or are willing to adjust to accommodate your needs. Whether you choose grilled instead of fried, ask for dressings on the side, or swap out carbs for extra veggies, there are plenty of ways to enjoy a meal without compromising your health.

Understanding the facts about diabetes and food can help you make better choices and confidently enjoy your meals. Remember, managing diabetes doesn't mean living by a long list of "don'ts." It's about finding balance, making informed decisions, and enjoying the foods that nourish your body and delight your taste buds.

UNDERSTANDING CARBOHYDRATES, SUGARS, AND GLYCEMIC INDEX

Let's discuss something super important when managing diabetes: carbohydrates, sugars, and the glycemic index. These are words you've probably heard often, but what do they mean, and why should you care? Don't worry — I'm here to break it down in a simple, easy-to-understand way.

What Are Carbohydrates?

Carbohydrates, or "carbs" for short, are one of the primary nutrients in our food. They're found in many different foods, from bread and pasta to fruits and vegetables. Carbs are your body's main energy source, significantly influencing your diet. But when you have diabetes, you need to pay extra attention to how many carbs you eat and what kinds you're choosing.

There are two main types of carbs:

- **Simple Carbohydrates:** These are sugars quickly absorbed by your body, which can cause your blood sugar to spike. Simple carbs are found in sugary drinks, candy, and baked goods made with white flour. Some simple carbs, like those in fruit and milk, also contain essential nutrients, so it's all about balance.
- **Complex Carbohydrates:** These are found in foods like whole grains, beans, and vegetables. They take longer for your body to break down, providing a more steady energy source and don't cause big spikes in blood sugar. Complex carbs are your friends when it comes to managing diabetes!

Understanding Sugars

When people talk about sugar, they usually mean the sweet stuff you add to your coffee or find in desserts. But sugar is a type of carbohydrate, and it's found naturally in many foods, like fruits, vegetables, and dairy. The sugar in a piece of fruit differs from that in a candy bar because it contains fiber, vitamins, and minerals that are good for you.

When you're managing diabetes, it's important to limit added sugars—those extra sugars that are put into foods during processing or preparation. These added sugars can cause quick spikes in your blood sugar and don't offer much nutrition. Instead, focus on getting your sugars from natural sources, like fruits, and enjoy sweets in moderation.

What Is the Glycemic Index (GI)?

The glycemic index (GI) is a tool for understanding how different foods affect blood sugar levels. Foods are ranked on a scale from 0 to 100 based on how quickly they raise blood sugar after you eat them.

The Glycemic Index Chart is a helpful tool that measures how quickly foods containing carbohydrates raise blood sugar levels. Foods are ranked on a scale from 0 to 100, with low GI foods being more slowly digested and absorbed, resulting in a gradual rise in blood sugar. This chart is designed to help you make informed choices for managing your diabetes.

GI Category	Food Items	GI Range
Low GI Foods	Non-Starchy Vegetables: Broccoli, spinach, cauliflower, cucumber, bell peppers, zucchini, leafy greens (e.g., kale, Swiss chard), asparagus, Brussels sprouts	10-20
	Legumes: Lentils, chickpeas, kidney beans, black beans, navy beans, split peas, soybeans	20-35
	Whole Grains: Steel-cut oats, quinoa, barley, bulgur, rye, farro, millet	45-55
	Fruits: Apples, pears, oranges, cherries, strawberries, peaches, plums, grapefruit, kiwifruit	30-45
	Dairy Products: Milk, plain yogurt, kefir, unsweetened almond milk, Greek yogurt (plain)	30-35
Medium GI Foods	Whole Wheat Bread, pita bread, multigrain bread, rye bread	55-65
	Basmati Rice, black rice, red rice	58
	Sweet Potatoes (boiled, baked)	60
	Bananas (ripe), mangoes	60
	Pineapple, figs, papaya	59
High GI Foods	White Bread, baguettes, bagels	75-85
	White Rice, sticky rice, jasmine rice	70-80
	Instant Oatmeal, quick-cooking oats	79
	Potatoes (baked or mashed), russet potatoes, French fries	80-90
	Watermelon, dates, parsnips	76

Tips for Managing GI in Your Diet

- **Choose Low GI Foods:** Opt for more low GI options to maintain steady blood sugar levels.
- **Combine Foods:** Pair high GI foods with low GI foods to lower the overall GI of a meal.
- **Watch Portions:** Even low GI foods can impact blood sugar if eaten in large quantities.

Understanding the GI of foods can help you build balanced meals that promote stable blood sugar levels and a healthy lifestyle.

Putting It All Together

Managing carbohydrates and sugars is vital to living well with diabetes. By choosing complex carbs, watching your intake of added sugars, and using the glycemic index as a guide, you can make smarter food choices that help keep your blood sugar in check.

But don't stress — this isn't about giving up all your favorite foods. It's about finding the right balance and making swaps that work for you. This cookbook is packed with recipes that show you how to enjoy tasty, satisfying meals while managing your carbs and sugars in a way that's good for your health.

STOCKING YOUR PANTRY: DIABETIC-FRIENDLY INGREDIENTS

A well-stocked pantry is like having a secret weapon in the kitchen. It makes it easy to whip up tasty, healthy meals without running to the store whenever you want to cook. When managing diabetes, having the right ingredients can help you make smart food choices and keep your blood sugar in check. Let's look at some diabetic-friendly ingredients you'll want to keep in your pantry.

1 Whole Grains

Whole grains are a fantastic source of fiber, which helps slow down the absorption of sugar into your bloodstream. They're also more nutritious than refined grains. Here are a few great options to keep on hand:

- **Quinoa:** A versatile, protein-packed grain that's perfect for salads, bowls, or as a side dish.
- **Brown Rice:** A hearty grain that's great for stir-fries, soups, or as a base for meals.
- **Oats:** Ideal for breakfast, overnight oats, or even healthy baking.
- **Whole Wheat Pasta:** A better alternative to regular pasta that adds fiber and nutrients to your dishes.

2 Legumes and Beans

Legumes and beans are rich in protein, fiber, and complex carbs, making them a fantastic choice for balanced meals. Plus, they're super filling! Stock up on:

- **Black Beans:** Perfect for salads, soups, and Mexican-inspired dishes.
- **Lentils:** Great for soups, stews, and veggie burgers.
- **Chickpeas:** Use them in salads, make hummus, or roast them for a crunchy snack.
- **Canned Beans:** Keep a few cans of low-sodium beans for quick, easy meals, and choose varieties with no added sugar.

3 Healthy Fats

Not all fats are created equal! Healthy fats are essential for heart health and can help keep you satisfied after meals. Here are some pantry staples:

- **Olive Oil:** Great for sautéing, roasting, or making salad dressings.
- **Avocado Oil:** Perfect for high-heat cooking and adds a mild, buttery flavor.
- **Nuts and Seeds:** Almonds, walnuts, chia seeds, and flaxseeds are all great for snacking or adding to recipes.
- **Nut Butters:** Look for natural, no-sugar-added options like almond or peanut butter.

4 Low-Glycemic Sweeteners

Managing diabetes doesn't mean you have to give up sweetness altogether! There are plenty of diabetic-friendly sweeteners that won't cause a significant spike in blood sugar:

- **Stevia:** A natural, calorie-free sweetener that's great for coffee, tea, and baking.
- **Monk Fruit Sweetener:** Another natural, no-calorie sweetener that's perfect for desserts and drinks.
- **Agave Nectar:** A lower-glycemic sweetener that can be used in moderation for baking or drizzling on foods.

5 Canned and Jarred Goods

These pantry staples are perfect for quick, healthy meals:

- **Canned Tomatoes:** Use them in soups, stews, and sauces. Make sure to choose varieties without added sugar to keep your meals diabetes-friendly.
- **Canned Tuna or Salmon:** Great for adding protein to salads or making sandwiches. Check the labels to ensure they're packed in water or olive oil without added sugars.
- **Low-Sodium Broth:** A base for soups, stews, and cooking grains. Look for no added sugar on the label.
- **Nut and Seed Butters:** Great for spreading on whole-grain toast or adding to smoothies. Always go for those without added sugar.

6 Spices and Herbs

Spices and herbs are the key to making healthy meals taste amazing! Plus, many herbs and spices offer health benefits of their own. Keep these in your pantry:

- **Cinnamon:** Adds warmth and sweetness to dishes without sugar.
- **Turmeric:** Known for its anti-inflammatory properties, it's great in soups, stews, and curries.
- **Cumin:** Adds depth to Mexican and Middle Eastern dishes.
- **Garlic Powder and Onion Powder:** Easy ways to add flavor without added calories or carbs.
- **Dried Herbs:** Basil, oregano, thyme, and rosemary are all versatile and delicious.

7 Vinegar and Sauces

A splash of vinegar or a drizzle of sauce can elevate a dish and add flavor without added sugar:

- **Apple Cider Vinegar:** Great for dressings, marinades, or even drinking with water for a refreshing drink.
- **Balsamic Vinegar:** Adds a rich, sweet flavor to salads and roasted veggies.
- **Soy Sauce (Low-Sodium):** Perfect for stir-fries and marinades. Opt for versions without added sugar.
- **Hot Sauce:** Adds heat and flavor to any dish without adding sugar.

8 Vegetables: Fresh, Frozen, and Canned

Vegetables are a cornerstone of any healthy diet and are especially important when managing diabetes. They're low in calories, high in fiber, and packed with essential vitamins and minerals. Here's how to keep your kitchen well-stocked with these nutrient powerhouses:

- **Fresh Vegetables:** Try to keep various fresh vegetables on hand whenever possible. Leafy greens like spinach and kale, cruciferous veggies like broccoli and cauliflower, and colorful options like bell peppers and carrots are all great. Fresh veggies are perfect for salads, stir-fries, and sides. If you're worried about them spoiling, buy what you know you'll use within a week and plan your meals around them.
- **Frozen Vegetables:** Frozen vegetables are just as nutritious as fresh ones and incredibly convenient. They're great to have on hand when you need a quick meal. Look for frozen spinach, broccoli, green beans, and mixed veggie blends. You can easily add them to soups, stews, and stir-fries or steam them as a side dish.
- **Canned Vegetables:** Canned vegetables are a great pantry staple because they last a long time and are ready to use immediately. Just be sure to choose low-sodium versions and, importantly, check the labels to ensure no added sugar. Canned tomatoes, green beans, corn, and peas are

versatile and can be added to various dishes. Please give them a quick rinse before using it to remove excess sodium.

- **Starchy Vegetables:** While starchy vegetables like sweet potatoes, butternut squash, and peas contain more carbs, they're still packed with nutrients and can be part of a balanced, diabetic-friendly diet. Just be mindful of portion sizes and pair them with lean protein and non-starchy vegetables for a well-rounded meal.

With these ingredients in your pantry, you'll be ready to tackle any recipe in this cookbook or devise your own healthy creations. Stocking your kitchen with these diabetic-friendly staples makes it easier to prepare meals that are delicious and good for managing your blood sugar.

So, take a little time to stock up, and cooking healthy meals at home becomes a breeze. Your pantry will become your best ally in your journey to better health!

UNDERSTANDING FOOD LABELS: WHAT TO LOOK FOR

Grocery shopping can feel like a bit of a puzzle sometimes, especially when trying to make healthy choices for managing diabetes. But here's the good news: learning to read food labels can make it much easier to find foods that are good for you and your blood sugar. Let's review the key things to look for on those labels, so you can shop confidently.

1 Start with the Serving Size

The serving size is the first thing you want to check on any food label. All the other information on the label—like calories, carbs, and sugars—is based on this amount. Sometimes, a package might look like a single serving, but when you check the label, you'll see it contains two or more servings. Knowing the serving size helps you understand how much you're eating.

2 Check the Total Carbohydrates

For managing diabetes, the total carbohydrate content is one of the most critical numbers on the label. This includes all types of carbs—sugars, fiber, and starches. Carbs significantly impact your blood sugar, so knowing how many grams you're getting per serving is essential. If comparing products, choose the one with lower total carbs or higher fiber.

3 Look at the Sugars

Right below total carbohydrates, you'll find sugars. This includes natural and added sugars (like those in fruit and milk). Added sugars are what you want to watch out for—they can cause your blood sugar to spike. Look for products with no added sugars and choose those with natural sugars instead. Some labels also show "Includes Xg Added Sugars," which makes it easier to see how much sugar has been added during processing.

4 Focus on Fiber

Fiber is your friend, especially when it comes to managing diabetes. It helps slow down how quickly your body absorbs sugar, which can help keep your blood sugar levels steady. The higher the fiber content, the better! Foods like whole grains, beans, and vegetables are excellent sources of fiber, so aim for products with a good amount of fiber.

5 Mind the Fat Content

Not all fats are bad, but it's important to be mindful of the type of fat in your food. Look for products low in saturated fats and free of trans fats, which can increase your risk of heart disease. Instead, choose foods with healthy fats, like nuts, seeds, and olive oil. Check the label to make sure you're getting the good kind!

6 Watch the Sodium

Too much sodium can raise your blood pressure, which is something you'll want to avoid, especially if you have diabetes. Processed foods often contain a lot of sodium, so look for low-sodium options and stay within the recommended limit of 2,300 milligrams—or 1,500 milligrams if you aim for optimal heart health. You can always season your food with herbs and spices at home instead!

7 Scan the Ingredients List

The ingredients list tells you what's really in your food. Ingredients are listed in order of quantity, so the first few ingredients make up most of the product. Keep an eye out for added sugars (which can appear under many names like high-fructose corn syrup, cane sugar, or honey) and unhealthy fats. If you see a lot of long, unpronounceable ingredients, it might be a sign that the food is highly processed. Look for whole, natural ingredients you recognize.

8 Consider the Calories

Calories aren't the only thing to consider, but they matter — especially if you're watching your weight. Remember, the calorie count on the label is for one serving, so if you eat more than that, you'll need to adjust the numbers accordingly. Balancing calorie intake with your activity level is critical to maintaining a healthy weight.

9 Choose Whole Foods When Possible

Whole foods, like fresh fruits and vegetables, whole grains, and lean proteins, often don't have a label—but they're some of the best choices you can make! When you choose packaged foods, try to pick those close to their natural state with minimal processing and additives.

10 Don't Be Fooled by "Healthy" Claims

Labels can be tricky, especially with all the "healthy" claims out there — like "low-fat," "sugar-free," or "all-natural." Just because a product says it's healthy doesn't necessarily mean it's the best choice. Always check the nutrition facts and ingredients list to get the whole story. For example, "sugar-free" might mean it's loaded with artificial sweeteners or other fillers.

Learning to read food labels is a powerful tool in your journey to manage diabetes and make healthier choices. It might take a little practice at first, but soon, you can scan a label and know whether a product fits your diet. Remember, it's all about balance — choosing nourishing and satisfying foods while keeping your blood sugar in check.

Next time you're at the store, take a moment to read those labels and make informed decisions. Your health is worth it!

PORTION CONTROL AND BALANCED MEALS

When managing diabetes, portion control and creating balanced meals are two of the most important things you can do. They help keep your blood sugar levels steady and ensure you get the proper nutrients to fuel your body. But don't worry — portion control doesn't mean you have to eat tiny amounts of food or feel hungry all the time. It's all about finding the right balance that works for you. Let's break it down together!

1 Why Portion Control Matters

Portion control is all about eating the right amount of food for your body's needs. When you overeat anything — even healthy foods—it can lead to spikes in blood sugar and unwanted weight gain, which can make managing diabetes more challenging. Conversely, eating too little can leave you unsatisfied and low energy. The goal is to find that sweet spot where you're eating just enough to feel full and energized without going overboard.

2 Understanding Serving Sizes

One of the easiest ways to practice portion control is by getting familiar with serving sizes. A serving size is a specific amount of food, often listed on the nutrition label, that helps you understand how much you're eating. Here's a guide using ounces and grams:

- **One serving of cooked rice or pasta** is about ½ cup, which equals approximately 4 ounces or 120 grams.
- **One serving of meat or fish** is about 3 ounces, roughly 85 grams.
- **One serving of non-starchy vegetables** is about 1 cup raw or ½ cup cooked, which equals approximately 3 ounces or 85 grams when cooked.
- **One serving of cheese** is about 1 ounce or roughly 28 grams.

Knowing these serving sizes can help you gauge how much food to put on your plate.

3 The Plate Method

A simple way to create balanced meals and control portions is to use the plate method. Here's how it works:

- **Fill half your plate with non-starchy vegetables** like leafy greens, broccoli, bell peppers, or cauliflower. Aim for about 6 ounces (170 grams) of these veggies. They're low in calories and carbs, so you can eat a generous portion without affecting your blood sugar.
- **Fill a quarter of your plate with lean protein** like chicken, fish, tofu, or beans. This should be about 3-4 ounces (85-113 grams). Protein helps keep you full and supports steady blood sugar levels.
- **Fill the last quarter of your plate with healthy carbohydrates** like whole grains, starchy vegetables (such as sweet potatoes), or fruit. Aim for 2-3 ounces (60-85 grams) or around ½ cup cooked. These carbs provide energy but are digested more slowly, helping to avoid blood sugar spikes.

This method helps you build a well-balanced meal that's satisfying and good for your blood sugar.

4 Mindful Eating

Portion control isn't just about what's on your plate — it's also about how you eat. Mindful eating means paying attention to your food, eating slowly, and enjoying each bite. This helps you tune in to your body's hunger and fullness cues, making you less likely to overeat. Avoid distractions like TV or your phone while eating, and take the time to savor your meal.

5 Snacking Wisely

Snacks can be a great way to keep your blood sugar levels stable between meals, but it's important to keep portions in check. Choose snacks that combine protein and healthy carbs, like a small apple with 1 tablespoon of peanut butter or a handful of nuts with some veggies. This balance helps keep you satisfied and prevents blood sugar spikes.

6 Be Aware of "Portion Distortion"

It's easy to get used to the oversized portions often served in restaurants or packaged foods, a phenomenon known as "portion distortion." When eating out, consider sharing a dish, asking for a half portion, or packing up half of your meal to take home. At home, try serving meals on smaller plates to help keep portions in check without feeling deprived.

7 Listen to Your Body

Your body is pretty good at telling you when it's had enough — if you listen. Eating slowly and mindfully helps you recognize when you're full and stop eating before feeling stuffed. Remember, leaving food on your plate or saving it for later if you're full is okay.

Portion control and balanced meals are powerful tools for managing diabetes and maintaining overall health. It's not about restricting yourself or going hungry—it's about enjoying various delicious foods in the right amounts. By focusing on portion sizes, using the plate method, and practicing mindful eating, you'll be well on your way to creating satisfying, nutritious meals that support your health goals.

COOKING METHODS TO RETAIN NUTRIENTS

When cooking healthy meals, how you cook your food is just as important as what you cook. Specific cooking methods can help retain the nutrients in your food, ensuring you're getting all the vitamins, minerals, and goodness your body needs — especially when managing diabetes. The good news is that cooking in a way that preserves nutrients doesn't have to be complicated. Let's dive into some easy and friendly tips to help you get the most out of your meals.

1 Steaming: A Gentle Approach

Steaming is one of the best ways to cook vegetables because it preserves their vitamins and minerals. By cooking your veggies with steam rather than water, you avoid losing nutrients that can leach out into the cooking liquid. Plus, steamed vegetables retain their bright color and natural flavor. You only need a steamer basket and a pot with water at the bottom. Cover and let the steam do the work!

2 Sautéing: Quick and Nutrient-Friendly

Sautéing is a quick and easy way to cook vegetables, lean meats, and seafood while retaining nutrients. You can lock in flavor and nutrients by cooking food over medium heat with a small amount of healthy oil (like olive oil or avocado oil). Just be careful not to overcook — keeping the heat moderate and the cooking time short will help preserve the vitamins in your food.

3 Roasting: Enhancing Flavor and Nutrition

Roasting is another excellent method that retains nutrients and brings out the natural sweetness in vegetables like carrots, sweet potatoes, and Brussels sprouts. Roasting at a moderate temperature (around 400°F or 200°C) with some oil helps vegetables caramelize while keeping most of their nutrients intact. Plus, it's super easy — toss your veggies on a baking sheet, pop them in the oven, and let them do their thing.

4 Grilling: A Tasty, Nutrient-Saving Method

Grilling is a fantastic way to cook lean meats, fish, and vegetables while retaining their nutrients and adding a delicious smoky flavor. Whether you're using an outdoor grill or an indoor grill pan, grilling is quick and uses high heat, which helps seal in the nutrients. Just be sure not to char your food too much, as overcooking can reduce the nutrient content.

5 Blanching: A Quick Nutrient Lock-In

Blanching involves briefly boiling vegetables and then plunging them into ice water to stop cooking. This method is great for retaining color, texture, and nutrients, especially when prepping vegetables for salads or freezing them for later use. It's also a quick way to cook veggies while preserving their vitamins.

6 Microwaving: Surprisingly Nutrient-Preserving

Microwaving gets a bad rap, but it's a great way to cook food quickly while retaining nutrients. Microwaving cooks food quickly with minimal water, and it helps preserve vitamins, especially those that are water-soluble like vitamin C. Just use a microwave-safe dish with a lid to steam your veggies or cook lean proteins.

7 Baking: A Versatile and Healthy Option

Baking is a versatile method that works well for savory dishes like fish and chicken and sweet treats like fruit crisps. Baking at a moderate temperature allows food to cook evenly while retaining moisture and nutrients. Plus, baking doesn't require a lot of added fat, making it a healthier option for preparing various dishes.

8 Avoid Boiling When Possible

Boiling can cause water-soluble vitamins like vitamins C and B to leach into the cooking water, especially if you're boiling for a long time. If you boil, try to use the cooking liquid in soups or sauces to recapture some of those lost nutrients. Or opt for steaming or sautéing, which are gentler on your food's nutritional content.

9 Keep It Simple: Less Is More

Sometimes, the best way to retain nutrients is to keep your cooking simple. Overcooking or using too much oil, butter, or sauces can mask the natural flavors of your food and reduce its nutritional value. Try to focus on fresh, whole ingredients and use minimal seasoning or dressing to let the natural goodness of your food shine through.

Putting It All Together

By choosing cooking methods that retain nutrients, you're making your meals healthier, more flavorful, and more satisfying. Whether steaming, roasting, grilling, or even microwaving, these techniques help you get the most out of your ingredients. Remember, the goal is to keep your food as close to its natural state as possible while still enjoying the process of cooking and eating.

SUBSTITUTING INGREDIENTS FOR LOWER SUGAR AND CARBS

One of the great things about cooking at home is that you have control over the ingredients you use. This means you can easily make swaps that lower the sugar and carbs in your meals, making them more diabetes-friendly without sacrificing flavor. These simple substitutions can help you enjoy your favorite dishes while keeping your blood sugar in check. Let's explore some easy and tasty swaps you can start using today!

1 Swap White Rice for Cauliflower Rice

White rice is a staple in many dishes but is high in carbs, which can spike blood sugar. A great alternative is cauliflower rice. It's low in carbs, high in fiber, and has a mild flavor that works well in stir-fries, burrito bowls, or as a side dish. You can buy it in the frozen section or make your own by grating or pulsing fresh cauliflower in a food processor.

2 Replace Regular Pasta with Zucchini Noodles or Whole Wheat Pasta

Traditional pasta is another high-carb food that can be easily substituted. Zucchini noodles (or "zoodles") are a fun, low-carb option that adds extra veggies. They're perfect for pairing with your favorite pasta sauce. If you prefer a more traditional texture, try whole wheat pasta or pasta made from legumes like chickpeas or lentils. These options are higher in fiber and protein, which helps keep your blood sugar stable.

3 Use Greek Yogurt Instead of Sour Cream or Mayonnaise

Greek yogurt is a fantastic substitute for sour cream or mayonnaise in recipes. It's creamy, tangy, and much lower in sugar and carbs. Plus, it's packed with protein, which can help keep you full longer. Use it in dips, dressings, or topping for tacos and baked potatoes.

4 Choose Spaghetti Squash Instead of Regular Spaghetti

If you're craving spaghetti but want to cut down on carbs, spaghetti squash is a great alternative. When cooked, the flesh of this squash separates into long, noodle-like strands that make a delicious and low-carb substitute for traditional pasta. Just toss it with your favorite sauce and get a satisfying, diabetes-friendly meal.

5 Opt for Almond Flour or Coconut Flour Instead of White Flour

When baking, swapping out white flour for almond flour or coconut flour can significantly reduce the carb content of your treats. Almond flour is high in protein and healthy fats, while coconut flour is fiber-rich. Both options are great for making everything from pancakes to cookies. Remember that these flours behave slightly differently than regular flour, so you may need to adjust your recipes slightly.

6   Sweeten with Stevia or Monk Fruit Instead of Sugar

If you need to sweeten a recipe, consider using natural, low-carb sweeteners like stevia or monk fruit instead of regular sugar. These sweeteners have little to no effect on blood sugar and can be used in cooking and baking. Just be sure to check the conversion chart on the packaging, as these sweeteners are often much sweeter than sugar, so you'll need less.

7   Swap Potatoes for Sweet Potatoes or Other Root Vegetables

While potatoes are high in carbs, sweet potatoes are a slightly better option with a lower glycemic index, meaning they have a slower effect on blood sugar. You can also try other root vegetables like turnips or parsnips, which can be roasted, mashed, or used in soups as a lower-carb alternative.

8   Replace Sugary Beverages with Infused Water or Herbal Tea

Sugary drinks can cause quick blood sugar spikes, so swapping them out for healthier options is a good idea. Infused water, made by adding fresh fruits, herbs, or cucumber slices to water, is a refreshing and low-sugar alternative. Herbal teas are another great option, offering a variety of flavors without the sugar.

9   Use Lettuce Wraps Instead of Bread or Tortillas

If you want to reduce carbs in your sandwiches or tacos, try using large lettuce leaves as wraps instead of bread or tortillas. They're crunchy, low in carbs, and add a fresh, light flavor to your meals. For a sturdy and nutritious wrap, you can use romaine, iceberg, or even collard greens.

10   Choose Berries Over High-Sugar Fruits

Fruits are a great source of vitamins and fiber, but some are higher in sugar than others. Berries, such as strawberries, blueberries, and raspberries, are lower in sugar and have a lower glycemic index than fruits like bananas or grapes. Enjoy them as a snack, in smoothies, or as a topping for yogurt or oatmeal.

Substituting ingredients to lower sugar and carbs in your meals is easier than you might think, and it doesn't mean you have to give up the foods you love. With these simple swaps, you can still enjoy delicious, satisfying meals that are better for your blood sugar. Plus, experimenting with these alternatives can introduce you to new flavors and textures you might love more than the originals!

CHAPTER 3

BREAKFAST RECIPES

Mornings can be busy, but it's important not to skip a healthy breakfast. A good breakfast sets the tone for your day, providing the energy and nutrients you need to stay focused and keep your blood sugar levels steady. In this section, you'll find quick and easy breakfast ideas that are both nutritious and delicious.

These recipes are designed to be simple and fast, so you can start your day right without spending too much time in the kitchen. Whether you prefer something sweet, savory, or somewhere in between, these breakfast options will help you kickstart your day confidently.

QUICK AND EASY BREAKFAST IDEAS

1

LOW-CARB EGG DISHES

Easy-to-make omelets, frittatas, and egg cups packed with veggies and lean proteins for a healthy start to your day.

2

WHOLE GRAIN BREAKFASTS

Wholesome breakfast options such as oatmeal, quinoa bowls, or whole grain toasts topped with nutrient-rich ingredients for sustained energy.

3

PROTEIN-PACKED SMOOTHIES

Nutritious smoothies featuring yogurt, fruits, and added protein are a quick and healthy way to start your day.

4

DIABETIC-FRIENDLY PANCAKES AND MUFFINS

Choose low-sugar, high-fiber options like almond or whole wheat flour pancakes and muffins for a healthy breakfast treat.

LOW-CARB EGG DISHES

TURKEY & BELL PEPPER MORNING BITES

Yield
2 servings (4 egg cups)

Preparation Time
10 minutes

Cooking Time
20 minutes

INGREDIENTS

- 3 large eggs
- 1/4 cup lean ground turkey, cooked and crumbled
- 1/4 cup diced bell peppers (any color)
- 2 tablespoons onion, finely chopped
- 2 tablespoons shredded cheddar cheese (optional)
- Salt and pepper to taste
- Cooking spray or muffin liners

DIRECTIONS

1. Preheat your oven to 350°F (175°C). Lightly grease a muffin tin with cooking spray or use muffin liners.
2. Whisk the eggs with a pinch of salt and pepper in a medium bowl.
3. Evenly divide the cooked ground turkey, diced bell peppers, and chopped onion among 4 muffin cups.
4. Pour the whisked eggs over the turkey and vegetables, filling each cup about 3/4 full. Sprinkle cheddar cheese on top if desired.
5. Bake for 18-20 minutes, or until the egg cups are set and lightly golden on top. Let cool for a few minutes before removing from the tin.

Nutritional Information: 160 calories, 12g protein, 3g carbohydrates, 9g fat, 1g fiber, 220mg cholesterol, 240mg sodium, 180mg potassium.

CREAMY AVOCADO & EGG POWER SCRAMBLE

Yield
2 servings

Preparation Time
5 minutes

Cooking Time
5 minutes

INGREDIENTS

- 4 large eggs
- 1 ripe avocado, diced
- 1/2 cup cherry tomatoes, halved
- 1 tablespoon olive oil
- 2 tablespoons fresh cilantro, chopped
- Salt and pepper to taste

DIRECTIONS

1. Whisk the eggs with a pinch of salt and pepper in a medium bowl.
2. Heat olive oil in a non-stick skillet over medium heat. Add the whisked eggs and cook, stirring gently, for 2-3 minutes until the eggs are soft and scrambled.
3. Once the eggs are cooked but still slightly soft, remove from heat and gently fold in the diced avocado and halved cherry tomatoes.
4. Garnish with fresh cilantro and serve immediately.

Nutritional Information: 280 calories, 14g protein, 9g carbohydrates, 23g fat, 6g fiber, 370mg cholesterol, 180mg sodium, 600mg potassium.

ZESTY ZUCCHINI & ONION FRITTATA

Yield
2 servings

Preparation Time
10 minutes

Cooking Time
15 Minutes

INGREDIENTS

- 4 large eggs
- 1 small zucchini, shredded
- 1/4 cup onion, finely chopped
- 1 tablespoon olive oil
- 1/4 teaspoon dried oregano (or any preferred herbs)
- Salt and pepper to taste
- Optional: fresh parsley for garnish

DIRECTIONS

1. Preheat the oven to 350°F (175°C).
2. Heat olive oil in an oven-safe skillet over medium heat. Add the chopped onion and cook for 3-4 minutes until softened.
3. Add the shredded zucchini to the skillet and cook for another 2-3 minutes until slightly tender. Season with salt, pepper, and dried oregano.
4. Whisk the eggs with a pinch of salt and pepper in a medium bowl. Pour the eggs over the zucchini and onion mixture into the skillet.
5. Cook for 2-3 minutes until the edges start to set, then transfer the skillet to the preheated oven.
6. Bake for 10-12 minutes until the eggs are fully set and the top is lightly golden. Garnish with fresh parsley, if desired, and serve warm.

Nutritional Information: 190 calories, 12g protein, 6g carbohydrates, 13g fat, 2g fiber, 370mg cholesterol, 180mg sodium, 400mg potassium.

BROCCOLI & CHEDDAR PROTEIN MUFFINS

Yield
2 servings (4 muffins)

Preparation Time
10 minutes

Cooking Time
20 minutes

INGREDIENTS

- 4 large eggs
- 1/2 cup chopped broccoli (fresh or frozen, thawed)
- 1/4 cup shredded low-fat cheddar cheese
- 1/4 teaspoon garlic powder (optional)
- Salt and pepper to taste
- Cooking spray or muffin liners

DIRECTIONS

1. Preheat your oven to 350°F (175°C). Lightly grease a muffin tin with cooking spray or use muffin liners.
2. In a medium bowl, whisk the eggs with a pinch of salt, pepper, and garlic powder (if using).
3. Evenly divide the chopped broccoli and shredded cheddar cheese among 4 muffin cups.
4. Pour the whisked eggs over the broccoli and cheese, filling each cup about 3/4 full.
5. Bake for 18-20 minutes or until the egg muffins are set and lightly golden on top. Let cool for a few minutes before removing from the tin.

Nutritional Information: 190 calories, 14g protein, 4g carbohydrates, 13g fat, 1g fiber, 220mg cholesterol, 280mg sodium, 200mg potassium.

SAVORY SPINACH & MUSHROOM DELIGHT OMELET

Yield

2 servings

Preparation Time

5 minutes

Cooking Time

10 Minutes

INGREDIENTS

- 4 large eggs
- 1/2 cup fresh spinach, chopped
- 1/2 cup mushrooms, sliced
- 1/4 cup feta cheese, crumbled
- 1 tablespoon olive oil
- Salt and pepper to taste
- Optional: fresh parsley for garnish

DIRECTIONS

1. Whisk the eggs with a pinch of salt and pepper in a medium bowl until well combined.
2. Heat olive oil in a non-stick skillet over medium heat. Add the sliced mushrooms and cook for 3-4 minutes until tender and slightly golden.
3. Add the chopped spinach to the skillet and cook for 1-2 minutes until wilted.
4. Pour the whisked eggs over the sautéed spinach and mushrooms, allowing them to spread evenly in the pan. Cook for 2-3 minutes, or until the eggs set around the edges.
5. Sprinkle the crumbled feta cheese on one half of the omelet. Gently fold the other half over the cheese and cook for another 1-2 minutes until the omelet is fully set and the cheese is slightly melted.
6. Serve warm, optionally garnished with fresh parsley

Nutritional Information: 220 calories, 15g protein, 5g carbohydrates, 15g fat, 2g fiber, 370mg cholesterol, 290mg sodium, 420mg potassium.

WHOLE GRAIN BREAKFASTS

CINNAMON-INFUSED APPLE QUINOA BOWL

Yield
2 servings

Preparation Time
5 minutes

Cooking Time
15 Minutes

INGREDIENTS

- 1/2 cup quinoa, rinsed
- 1 cup water
- 1/2 cup unsweetened almond milk (or any preferred milk)
- 1 small apple, diced
- 1/2 teaspoon ground cinnamon
- 1 tablespoon chopped walnuts
- 1 teaspoon honey or agave syrup (optional)

DIRECTIONS

1. Combine the rinsed quinoa and water in a medium saucepan. Bring to a boil over medium heat, then reduce the heat to low, cover, and simmer for 12-15 minutes until the quinoa is cooked and the water is absorbed.
2. Stir in the almond milk, diced apple, and ground cinnamon. Cook for an additional 2-3 minutes until the apple softens and the mixture is warmed through.
3. Divide the quinoa mixture between two bowls. Top with chopped walnuts and drizzle with honey or agave syrup if desired.

Nutritional Information: 240 calories, 6g protein, 39g carbohydrates, 8g fat, 4g fiber, 0mg cholesterol, 50mg sodium, 340mg potassium.

PEANUT BUTTER BANANA DREAM OATMEAL

Yield
2 servings

Preparation Time
5 minutes

Cooking Time
5 minutes

INGREDIENTS

- 1 cup rolled oats
- 2 cups water
- 1/2 cup unsweetened almond milk (to stir in after cooking)
- 1 medium banana, sliced
- 2 tablespoons natural peanut butter
- 1/2 teaspoon ground cinnamon (optional)
- 1 teaspoon honey or agave syrup (optional)

DIRECTIONS

1. In a medium saucepan, bring the water to a boil. Stir in the rolled oats, reduce the heat to low, and simmer for 5 minutes, stirring occasionally until the oats are soft and creamy.
2. Remove the oatmeal from heat and stir in the almond milk to add creaminess.
3. Divide the oatmeal into two bowls. Top each with sliced banana and drizzle with 1 tablespoon of peanut butter.
4. Sprinkle with cinnamon and drizzle with honey or agave syrup if desired. Serve warmly.

Nutritional Information: 300 calories, 9g protein, 44g carbohydrates, 12g fat, 7g fiber, 0mg cholesterol, 70mg sodium, 390mg potassium.

AVOCADO & TOMATO GOODNESS TOAST

Yield
2 servings

Preparation Time
5 minutes

Cooking Time
2 Minutes

INGREDIENTS

- 2 slices whole wheat bread, toasted
- 1 ripe avocado
- 1 small tomato, sliced
- Salt and pepper to taste

Optional: a squeeze of lemon juice or red pepper flakes

DIRECTIONS

1. Toast the whole wheat bread slices until golden and crisp.
2. Cut the avocado in half while the bread is toasting. Remove the pit and scoop the flesh into a small bowl. Mash the avocado with a fork until smooth. Season with salt, pepper, and a squeeze of lemon juice (if desired).
3. Spread the mashed avocado evenly over the toasted bread slices.
4. Top each toast with sliced tomato and season with a pinch of salt and pepper. Add optional toppings like red pepper flakes for extra flavor if desired.
5. Serve immediately.

Nutritional Information: 250 calories, 6g protein, 26g carbohydrates, 15g fat, 8g fiber, 0mg cholesterol, 220mg sodium, 650mg potassium.

BLUEBERRY ALMOND BLISS OVERNIGHT OATS

Yield
2 servings

Preparation Time
5 minutes

Cooking Time
0 minutes

INGREDIENTS

- 1 cup rolled oats
- 1 cup unsweetened almond milk
- 1/2 cup fresh or frozen blueberries
- 2 tablespoons sliced almonds
- 1 tablespoon chia seeds (optional)
- 1 teaspoon honey or agave syrup (optional)

DIRECTIONS

1. In a medium bowl or two jars, combine the rolled oats, almond milk, chia seeds (if using), and honey or agave syrup (if desired). Stir well to combine.
2. Cover and refrigerate overnight, or for at least 4 hours, to allow the oats to soften and absorb the liquid.
3. When ready to serve, stir the oats and top each serving with fresh blueberries and sliced almonds.
4. Serve chilled or at room temperature.

Nutritional Information: 240 calories, 7g protein, 40g carbohydrates, 9g fat, 7g fiber, 0mg cholesterol, 70mg sodium, 350mg potassium.

SWEET POTATO SUNRISE QUINOA BOWL

Yield
2 servings

Preparation Time
10 minutes

Cooking Time
30 Minutes

INGREDIENTS

- 1/2 cup quinoa, rinsed
- 1 small sweet potato, peeled and diced
- 2 large eggs (poached)
- 1 tablespoon olive oil
- Salt and pepper to taste
- 1/2 teaspoon paprika (optional)
- Fresh parsley or cilantro for garnish (optional)

DIRECTIONS

1. Preheat the oven to 400°F (200°C). Toss the diced sweet potato with olive oil, salt, pepper, and paprika (if using). Spread on a baking sheet and roast for 20-25 minutes or until tender and slightly crispy.

2. While the sweet potato is roasting, cook the quinoa. In a medium saucepan, bring 1 cup of water to a boil. Add the quinoa, reduce the heat to low, cover, and simmer for 12-15 minutes until the quinoa is cooked and the water is absorbed. Fluff with a fork.

3. Poach the eggs by bringing a pot of water to a gentle simmer. Crack each egg into a small bowl and gently slide them into the simmering water. Cook for 3-4 minutes until the whites are set, but the yolks are still runny. Remove with a slotted spoon.

4. Divide the cooked quinoa between two bowls. Top each bowl with roasted sweet potatoes and a poached egg. Garnish with fresh parsley or cilantro, and season with additional salt and pepper.

Nutritional Information: 340 calories, 13g protein, 42g carbohydrates, 14g fat, 6g fiber, 190mg cholesterol, 230mg sodium, 660mg potassium.

PROTEIN-PACKED SMOOTHIES

BERRY BLISS PROTEIN SMOOTHIE

Yield
2 servings

Preparation Time
5 minutes

Cooking Time
0 minutes

INGREDIENTS

- 1 cup mixed berries (fresh or frozen)
- 1/2 cup plain Greek yogurt
- 1/2 cup unsweetened almond milk (or any preferred milk)
- 1 tablespoon chia seeds (optional)
- 1/2 teaspoon vanilla extract (optional)
- 1-2 teaspoons honey or agave syrup (optional)

DIRECTIONS

1. In a blender, combine the mixed berries, Greek yogurt, almond milk, chia seeds (if using), and vanilla extract (if using).
2. Blend on high until smooth and creamy. If the smoothie is too thick, add more almond milk to reach your desired consistency.
3. Taste and add honey or agave syrup for extra sweetness if needed.
4. Pour into two glasses and serve immediately.

Nutritional Information: 160 calories, 10g protein, 22g carbohydrates, 4g fat, 5g fiber, 5mg cholesterol, 60mg sodium, 250mg potassium.

GREEN POWERHOUSE PEANUT BUTTER SMOOTHIE

Yield
2 servings

Preparation Time
5 minutes

Cooking Time
0 minutes

INGREDIENTS

- 1 cup fresh spinach
- 1/2 cup unsweetened almond milk (or any preferred milk)
- 1/2 cup plain Greek yogurt
- 1 tablespoon natural peanut butter
- 1/2 banana, sliced
- 1 tablespoon chia seeds (optional)
- 1/2 teaspoon vanilla extract (optional)

DIRECTIONS

1. Blend the spinach, almond milk, Greek yogurt, peanut butter, banana, chia seeds (if using), and vanilla extract.
2. Blend on high until smooth and creamy. Add more almond milk if needed to adjust the consistency.
3. Pour into two glasses and serve immediately.

Nutritional Information: 220 calories, 12g protein, 22g carbohydrates, 11g fat, 5g fiber, 5mg cholesterol, 120mg sodium, 490mg potassium.

BANANA BOOST PROTEIN SHAKE

Yield
2 servings

Preparation Time
5 minutes

Cooking Time
0 Minutes

INGREDIENTS

- 1 medium banana
- 1 tablespoon almond butter
- 1 scoop vanilla protein powder
- 1 cup unsweetened almond milk (or any preferred milk)
- 1/2 teaspoon cinnamon (optional)
- 1/2 cup ice cubes (optional, for a thicker shake)

DIRECTIONS

1. In a blender, combine the banana, almond butter, protein powder, almond milk, and cinnamon (if using).
2. Blend on high until smooth and creamy. Add ice cubes if you prefer a thicker, colder shake, and blend again.
3. Pour into two glasses and enjoy immediately.

Nutritional Information: 250 calories, 20g protein, 24g carbohydrates, 9g fat, 4g fiber, 0mg cholesterol, 220mg sodium, 400mg potassium.

STRAWBERRY-CUCUMBER REFRESHER

Yield
2 servings

Preparation Time
5 minutes

Cooking Time
0 minutes

INGREDIENTS

- 1 cup fresh or frozen strawberries
- 1/2 cup cucumber, peeled and chopped
- 1 cup unsweetened coconut water (or water)
- 1 tablespoon lime juice (freshly squeezed)
- 1 teaspoon agave syrup (optional for extra sweetness)
- 1/2 cup ice cubes (optional)

DIRECTIONS

1. In a blender, combine the strawberries, cucumber, coconut water, lime juice, and honey (if using).
2. Blend on high until smooth and well combined. Add ice cubes and blend again for a colder, more refreshing smoothie.
3. Pour into two glasses and serve immediately.

Nutritional Information: 80 calories, 1g protein, 20g carbohydrates, 0.5g fat, 3g fiber, 0mg cholesterol, 40mg sodium, 240mg potassium.

CHOCOLATE CHIA DREAM SMOOTHIE

Yield
2 servings

Preparation Time
5 minutes

Cooking Time
0 Minutes

INGREDIENTS

- 1 cup unsweetened almond milk (or any preferred milk)
- 1/2 cup plain Greek yogurt
- 1 tablespoon unsweetened cocoa powder
- 1 tablespoon chia seeds
- 1 tablespoon honey or agave syrup (optional)
- 1/2 teaspoon vanilla extract (optional)
- 1/2 cup ice cubes (optional for a thicker smoothie)

DIRECTIONS

1. Combine the almond milk, Greek yogurt, cocoa powder, chia seeds, honey (if using), and vanilla extract in a blender.
2. Blend on high until smooth and creamy. Add ice cubes for a thicker, colder smoothie and blend again.
3. Pour into two glasses and serve immediately.

Nutritional Information: 180 calories, 9g protein, 20g carbohydrates, 7g fat, 5g fiber, 5mg cholesterol, 90mg sodium, 290mg potassium.

DIABETIC-FRIENDLY PANCAKES AND MUFFINS

ALMOND FLOUR BERRY BURST PANCAKES

INGREDIENTS

- 1 cup almond flour
- 2 large eggs
- 1/4 cup unsweetened almond milk (or any preferred milk)
- 1/2 teaspoon baking powder
- 1/2 teaspoon vanilla extract (optional)
- 1/2 cup fresh mixed berries (blueberries, raspberries, or strawberries)
- 1 tablespoon butter or cooking spray (for cooking)
- Optional: a drizzle of sugar-free syrup or a sprinkle of powdered erythritol for serving

Yield
2 servings

Preparation Time
5 minutes

Cooking Time
10 Minutes

DIRECTIONS

1. In a medium bowl, whisk together the almond flour, eggs, almond milk, baking powder, and vanilla extract (if using) until the batter is smooth.
2. Heat a non-stick skillet or griddle over medium heat and lightly grease it with butter or cooking spray.
3. Pour about 1/4 cup of batter onto the skillet for each pancake. Cook for 2-3 minutes until bubbles start forming on the surface, then flip and cook for another 2-3 minutes until golden brown.
4. Serve the pancakes warm, topped with fresh berries and an optional drizzle of sugar-free syrup.

Nutritional Information: 250 calories, 12g protein, 10g carbohydrates, 19g fat, 5g fiber, 110mg cholesterol, 190mg sodium, 220mg potassium.

CINNAMON SPICE ALMOND PANCAKES

INGREDIENTS

- 1 cup almond flour
- 2 large eggs
- 1/4 cup unsweetened almond milk (or any preferred milk)
- 1/2 teaspoon baking powder
- 1/2 teaspoon ground cinnamon
- 1 teaspoon vanilla extract (optional)
- 1tablespoon chopped walnuts (for topping)
- 1 tablespoon butter or cooking spray (for cooking)
- Optional: sugar-free syrup or a drizzle of honey for serving

Yield
2 servings

Preparation Time
5 minutes

Cooking Time
10 Minutes

DIRECTIONS

1. In a medium bowl, whisk together the almond flour, eggs, almond milk, baking powder, cinnamon, and vanilla extract (if using) until smooth.
2. Heat a non-stick skillet or griddle over medium heat and lightly grease it with butter or cooking spray.
3. Pour about 1/4 cup of the batter onto the skillet for each pancake. Cook for 2-3 minutes on one side until bubbles form, then flip and cook for another 2-3 minutes until golden brown.
4. Serve the pancakes warm, topped with chopped walnuts and a drizzle of sugar-free syrup or honey if desired.

Nutritional Information: 280 calories, 14g protein, 9g carbohydrates, 22g fat, 5g fiber, 110mg cholesterol, 150mg sodium, 300mg potassium.

BANANA NUT MORNING MUFFINS

Yield
6 muffins

Preparation Time
10 minutes

Cooking Time
20 minutes

INGREDIENTS

- 1 cup whole wheat flour
- 1/2 teaspoon baking soda
- 1/2 teaspoon baking powder
- 1/4 teaspoon ground cinnamon (optional)
- 2 ripe bananas, mashed
- 1 large egg
- 1/4 cup unsweetened applesauce
- 1/4 cup chopped walnuts
- 1 teaspoon vanilla extract (optional)

DIRECTIONS

1. Preheat your oven to 350°F (175°C) and line a muffin tin with 6 paper liners or lightly grease with cooking spray.
2. In a medium bowl, whisk together the whole wheat flour, baking soda, baking powder, and cinnamon (if using).
3. Mix the mashed bananas, egg, unsweetened applesauce, and vanilla extract in another bowl until well combined.
4. Add the wet ingredients to the dry ingredients and stir until just combined. Fold in the chopped walnuts.
5. Divide the batter evenly among the 6 muffin cups. Bake for 18-20 minutes or until a toothpick inserted into the center comes clean.
6. Let the muffins cool slightly before serving.

Nutritional Information: 160 calories, 5g protein, 28g carbohydrates, 5g fat, 4g fiber, 35mg cholesterol, 90mg sodium, 240mg potassium.

OAT & FLAX POWER PANCAKES

Yield
2 servings

Preparation Time
5 minutes

Cooking Time
10 Minutes

INGREDIENTS

- 1/2 cup rolled oats
- 2 tablespoons ground flaxseed
- 1/2 cup unsweetened almond milk (or any preferred milk)
- 1 large egg
- 1/2 teaspoon baking powder
- 1/4 teaspoon ground cinnamon (optional)
- 1 teaspoon vanilla extract (optional)
- 1 tablespoon olive oil or cooking spray (for cooking)

DIRECTIONS

1. Combine the rolled oats, ground flaxseed, almond milk, egg, baking powder, cinnamon, and vanilla extract in a blender. Blend until smooth and let the batter rest for a minute to thicken slightly.
2. Heat a non-stick skillet or griddle over medium heat and lightly grease it with olive oil or cooking spray.
3. Pour about 1/4 cup of batter onto the skillet for each pancake. Cook for 2-3 minutes or until bubbles form on the surface. Flip and cook for another 2-3 minutes until golden brown.
4. Serve warm, topped with fresh fruit or a drizzle of sugar-free syrup if desired.

Nutritional Information: 210 calories, 8g protein, 24g carbohydrates, 10g fat, 6g fiber, 55mg cholesterol, 150mg sodium, 260mg potassium.

ZESTY LEMON-BLUEBERRY MUFFINS

Yield

6 muffins

Preparation Time

10 minutes

Cooking Time

20 minutes

INGREDIENTS

- 1 cup whole wheat flour
- 1/2 teaspoon baking powder
- 1/4 teaspoon baking soda
- 1/4 teaspoon salt
- 1 large egg
- 1/4 cup unsweetened applesauce
- 1/4 cup almond milk (or any preferred milk)
- 1/4 cup honey or agave syrup (optional, for added sweetness)
- 1 teaspoon vanilla extract
- Zest of 1 lemon
- 1/2 cup fresh or frozen blueberries

DIRECTIONS

1. Preheat your oven to 350°F (175°C) and line a muffin tin with 6 paper liners or lightly grease with cooking spray.
2. In a medium bowl, whisk together the whole wheat flour, baking powder, baking soda, and salt.
3. In another bowl, whisk the egg, unsweetened applesauce, almond milk, honey (if using), vanilla extract, and lemon zest.
4. Add the wet and dry ingredients and stir until just combined. Gently fold in the blueberries.
5. Divide the batter evenly among the 6 muffin cups. Bake for 18-20 minutes or until a toothpick inserted into the center comes clean.
6. Let the muffins cool for a few minutes before serving.

Nutritional Information: 160 calories, 4g protein, 30g carbohydrates, 3g fat, 4g fiber, 35mg cholesterol, 130mg sodium, 200mg potassium.

CHAPTER 4

LUNCH RECIPES

Eating lunch is important for keeping your energy levels steady and your blood sugar balanced, especially if you have diabetes. A well-balanced lunch provides the nutrients you need to stay focused and productive while also preventing energy dips and blood sugar spikes later in the day. Lunch doesn't have to be difficult, even if you have diabetes. You can enjoy a healthy and satisfying meal with suitable recipes without spending much time in the kitchen. In this section, you'll find various quick and easy lunch ideas that are delicious and suitable for diabetes.

These recipes use simple ingredients and easy preparation to energize you throughout the day. Whether at home or taking a meal on the go, these lunch options will help you stay on track with your health goals while enjoying your food.

QUICK AND EASY LUNCH IDEAS

1

POWER GREENS AND PROTEIN BOWLS

These easy-to-make bowls feature affordable greens like spinach, romaine, or kale paired with budget-friendly proteins like canned tuna, rotisserie chicken, or boiled eggs.

2

BUDGET-FRIENDLY GRAIN-FREE LUNCHES

Simple and affordable grain-free options use basic ingredients like cauliflower rice, zucchini noodles, or black beans to keep lunches low-carb and satisfying.

3

MEDITERRANEAN-INSPIRED WRAPS AND BOWLS

Flavorful Mediterranean lunches made with everyday staples like canned chickpeas, olives, cucumbers, and whole wheat wraps, drizzled with olive oil and lemon.

4

ONE-PAN VEGGIE-PACKED SKILLETS

Quick and hearty one-pan meals with affordable veggies like bell peppers, onions, and carrots, paired with protein options like ground turkey or tofu for a warm and nourishing lunch.

POWER GREENS AND PROTEIN BOWLS

ROMAINE & ROTISSERIE CHICKEN SALAD

INGREDIENTS

- 4 cups chopped romaine lettuce
- 1 cup shredded rotisserie chicken
- 1/2 avocado, sliced
- 1/2 cucumber, thinly sliced
- 1/4 cup cherry tomatoes, halved
- 1/4 cup crumbled feta cheese
- 1/4 cup roasted pumpkin seeds (optional)
- 2 tablespoons olive oil
- 1 tablespoon balsamic vinegar
- 1 teaspoon Dijon mustard
- 1 teaspoon lemon juice
- Salt and pepper to taste

Yield
2 servings

Preparation Time
10 minutes

Cooking Time
0 Minutes

DIRECTIONS

1. Prepare the Dressing. In a small bowl, whisk together olive oil, balsamic vinegar, Dijon mustard, lemon juice, and a pinch of salt and pepper to create a zesty vinaigrette.
2. Divide the chopped romaine lettuce between two bowls. Top each bowl with shredded rotisserie chicken, avocado slices, cucumber, cherry tomatoes, and crumbled feta cheese.
3. Sprinkle roasted pumpkin seeds over each bowl for added crunch and texture.
4. Drizzle the prepared vinaigrette over each salad. Toss lightly, adjust seasoning with salt and pepper if needed, and serve immediately.

Nutritional Information: 410 calories, 25g protein, 14g carbohydrates, 30g fat, 7g fiber, 70mg cholesterol, 340mg sodium, 850mg potassium.

SPINACH & BLACK BEAN PROTEIN BOWL

INGREDIENTS

- 4 cups fresh spinach
- 1 cup canned black beans, drained and rinsed
- 1/2 red bell pepper, diced
- 1/2 avocado, diced
- 1/4 cup shredded cheddar cheese (or your preferred cheese)
- 1/4 cup salsa (store-bought or homemade)
- 2 tablespoons sour cream (optional)
- 1 tablespoon fresh cilantro, chopped (optional)
- 1 tablespoon lime juice
- Salt and pepper to taste

Yield
2 servings

Preparation Time
10 minutes

Cooking Time
0 Minutes

DIRECTIONS

1. Divide the fresh spinach between two bowls. Top each bowl with half of the black beans, bell pepper, and avocado.
2. Sprinkle shredded cheddar cheese over the top of each bowl. Spoon the salsa over the salad for flavor.
3. Drizzle with lime juice and add a dollop of sour cream if desired. Sprinkle with fresh cilantro, and season with salt and pepper to taste.
4. Toss lightly and serve immediately.

Nutritional Information: 320 calories, 15g protein, 27g carbohydrates, 18g fat, 10g fiber, 20mg cholesterol, 460mg sodium, 900mg potassium.

KALE & HARD-BOILED EGG POWER BOWL

INGREDIENTS

- 4 cups kale, stems removed and chopped
- 2 hard-boiled eggs, sliced
- 1/2 avocado, sliced
- 1/4 cup red onion, thinly sliced
- 1/4 cup crumbled feta cheese
- 1/4 cup cherry tomatoes, halved
- 2 tablespoons toasted sunflower seeds (optional)
- 2 tablespoons olive oil
- 1 tablespoon apple cider vinegar (or balsamic vinegar)
- 1 teaspoon Dijon mustard
- 1 teaspoon honey (optional)
- Salt and pepper to taste

Yield
2 servings

Preparation Time
10 minutes

Cooking Time
10 Minutes

DIRECTIONS

1. In a large bowl, massage the chopped kale with 1 tablespoon of olive oil and a pinch of salt for 1-2 minutes until the kale softens and becomes tender.
2. Prepare the Dressing. In a small bowl, whisk together the remaining olive oil, apple cider vinegar, Dijon mustard, honey (if using), and a pinch of salt and pepper to create a tangy vinaigrette.
3. Divide the massaged kale between two bowls. Top each bowl with sliced hard-boiled eggs, avocado slices, cherry tomatoes, red onion slices, crumbled feta, and toasted sunflower seeds for added crunch.
4. Drizzle the prepared vinaigrette over each bowl. Toss lightly, season with additional salt and pepper if desired, and serve immediately.

Nutritional Information: 380 calories, 14g protein, 17g carbohydrates, 30g fat, 7g fiber, 190mg cholesterol, 350mg sodium, 700mg potassium.

CHICKEN & ARUGULA POWER BOWL

INGREDIENTS

- 2 boneless, skinless chicken breasts
- 1 tablespoon olive oil, plus more for drizzling
- Salt and pepper to taste
- 4 cups fresh arugula
- 1 cup cherry tomatoes, halved
- 1 cucumber, thinly sliced
- 1/2 cup hummus (store-bought or homemade)
- 1/4 teaspoon dried oregano (optional)
- Lemon wedges for serving (optional)

Yield
2 servings

Preparation Time
15 minutes

Cooking Time
15 Minutes

DIRECTIONS

1. Grill the Chicken. Preheat a grill or grill pan over medium-high heat. Drizzle the chicken breasts with 1 tablespoon of olive oil and season with salt, pepper, and oregano (if using). Grill the chicken for 6-7 minutes per side or until fully cooked and the internal temperature reaches 165°F (74°C). Remove from the grill and let rest for a few minutes before slicing.
2. Divide the arugula between two bowls. Top each with half the grilled chicken, cherry tomatoes, and cucumber slices.
3. Add a generous scoop of hummus to each bowl. Drizzle with olive oil and squeeze lemon juice over the top if desired.
4. Serve immediately, enjoying this healthy power bowl's vibrant flavors and fresh ingredients.

Nutritional Information: 350 calories, 30g protein, 15g carbohydrates, 18g fat, 6g fiber, 75mg cholesterol, 400mg sodium, 800mg potassium.

TUNA & SPINACH POWER BOWL

Yield

2 servings

Preparation Time

10 minutes

Cooking Time

10 minutes

INGREDIENTS

- 4 cups fresh spinach
- 1 can (5 oz) tuna in water, drained
- 1/2 avocado, sliced
- 1/4 cup cherry tomatoes, halved
- 1/4 cup cucumber, diced
- 2 tablespoons olives, sliced (optional)
- 2 tablespoons toasted sunflower seeds or pumpkin seeds
- 1 tablespoon capers (optional, for extra tang)
- 2 tablespoons olive oil
- 1 tablespoon lemon juice
- 1 teaspoon Dijon mustard
- 1/2 teaspoon honey (optional)
- Salt and pepper to taste

DIRECTIONS

1. Prepare the Dressing. Whisk together the olive oil, lemon juice, Dijon mustard, honey (if using), and a pinch of salt and pepper in a small bowl.

2. Divide the fresh spinach between two bowls. Top each with half the drained tuna, avocado slices, cherry tomatoes, cucumber, olives, sunflower seeds, and capers for added texture and tang.

3. Drizzle the prepared dressing over each bowl. Toss lightly, adjust seasoning with more salt and pepper, and serve immediately.

Nutritional Information: 370 calories, 28g protein, 14g carbohydrates, 25g fat, 6g fiber, 55mg cholesterol, 460mg sodium, 900mg potassium.

BUDGET-FRIENDLY GRAIN-FREE LUNCHES

CAULIFLOWER RICE & TOFU STIR-FRY

INGREDIENTS

- 1 cup cauliflower rice (store-bought or homemade)
- 1 block (8 oz) firm tofu, cubed
- 1 bell pepper, diced
- 1/2 onion, diced
- 2 cloves garlic, minced
- 2 tablespoons soy sauce (low sodium)
- 1 tablespoon olive oil or sesame oil (for cooking)
- 1/2 teaspoon ground ginger (optional)
- 1 tablespoon green onions, chopped (for garnish)
- 1 tablespoon sesame seeds (optional, for garnish)
- Salt and pepper to taste

Yield
2 servings

Preparation Time
15 minutes

Cooking Time
15 Minutes

DIRECTIONS

1. Heat 1 tablespoon of oil in a large skillet over medium heat. Add the cubed tofu and cook for 5-7 minutes, flipping occasionally, until crispy and golden on all sides. Remove tofu from the skillet and set aside.
2. Add the diced onion, bell pepper, and minced garlic in the same skillet. Sauté for 3-4 minutes until the vegetables begin to soften.
3. Add the cauliflower rice to the skillet and cook for another 3-5 minutes, stirring frequently, until tender. Add the soy sauce and ground ginger and stir to combine.
4. Return the crispy tofu to the skillet and toss everything together. Cook for an additional 2 minutes to allow the flavors to meld.
5. Remove from heat and garnish with chopped green onions and sesame seeds. Season with salt and pepper to taste. Serve hot.

Nutritional Information: 280 calories, 14g protein, 18g carbohydrates, 16g fat, 6g fiber, 0mg cholesterol, 600mg sodium, 500mg potassium.

BLACK BEAN & AVOCADO SALAD

INGREDIENTS

- 1 cup canned black beans, drained and rinsed
- 1 ripe avocado, diced
- 1/2 cup cherry tomatoes, halved
- 1/4 cup red onion, finely diced
- 2 tablespoons fresh cilantro, chopped
- 1 tablespoon olive oil
- 1 tablespoon lime juice
- Salt and pepper to taste

Yield
2 servings

Preparation Time
10 minutes

Cooking Time
0 Minutes

DIRECTIONS

1. In a medium bowl, combine the black beans, diced avocado, cherry tomatoes, red onion, and cilantro.
2. Drizzle the olive oil and lime juice over the salad. Gently toss everything together to coat the ingredients evenly.
3. Season with salt and pepper to taste. Serve immediately.

Nutritional Information: 290 calories, 9g protein, 25g carbohydrates, 19g fat, 11g fiber, 0mg cholesterol, 240mg sodium, 700mg potassium.

EGGPLANT & CAULIFLOWER CURRY

INGREDIENTS

- 1 large eggplant, diced
- 1 small head of cauliflower, cut into florets
- 2 tablespoons olive oil
- 1 onion, finely chopped
- 3 cloves garlic, minced
- 1 tablespoon fresh ginger, minced
- 2 tablespoons curry powder
- 1 teaspoon ground cumin
- 1/2 teaspoon ground turmeric
- 1 can (14.5 oz) diced tomatoes
- 1 can (13.5 oz) coconut milk
- Salt and pepper to taste
- Fresh cilantro for garnish (optional)
- Cooked brown rice or naan bread for serving (optional)

Yield
4 servings

Preparation Time
15 minutes

Cooking Time
30 Minutes

DIRECTIONS

1. Prepare the vegetables. Heat the olive oil over medium heat in a large pot or deep skillet. Add the chopped onion and sauté for about 5 minutes until softened. Add the minced garlic and ginger, cooking for another 1-2 minutes until fragrant.
2. Stir in the curry powder, ground cumin, and turmeric, allowing the spices to cook for about 1 minute. Add the diced eggplant and cauliflower florets, stirring to coat the vegetables with the spices.
3. Simmer the curry. Pour in the diced tomatoes (with their juice) and coconut milk. Stir well to combine. Season with salt and pepper to taste. Bring the mixture to a simmer, then reduce the heat to low. Cover and cook for 20-25 minutes until the eggplant and cauliflower are tender.
4. Serve the curry hot, garnished with fresh cilantro if desired. For a complete meal, enjoy with cooked brown rice or naan bread.

Nutritional Information: 320 calories, 5g protein, 22g carbohydrates, 24g fat, 7g fiber, 0mg cholesterol, 450mg sodium, 700mg potassium.

RED LENTIL & VEGGIE BOWL

INGREDIENTS

- 1/2 cup dried red lentils
- 1 1/2 cups water
- 1/2 onion, diced
- 1 carrot, diced
- 1/2 bell pepper, diced
- 1 clove garlic, minced
- 1 tablespoon olive oil
- 1/2 teaspoon cumin
- 1/4 teaspoon smoked paprika (optional)
- 1 tablespoon lemon juice
- Salt and pepper to taste
- Fresh parsley or cilantro for garnish (optional)

Yield
2 servings

Preparation Time
10 minutes

Cooking Time
15 Minutes

DIRECTIONS

1. Cook the lentils. Combine the red lentils and water in a medium saucepan. Bring to a boil, then reduce heat and simmer for 10-12 minutes until the lentils are tender but not mushy. Drain any excess water.
2. While the lentils are cooking, heat the olive oil in a large skillet over medium heat. Add the diced onion, carrot, bell pepper, and garlic. Sauté for 5-7 minutes until the vegetables are tender.
3. Add the cooked red lentils to the skillet with the sautéed vegetables. Stir in the cumin, smoked paprika (if using), lemon juice, salt, and pepper. Cook for another 2-3 minutes to blend the flavors.
4. Divide the red lentil and veggie mixture between two bowls. Garnish with fresh parsley or cilantro if desired. Serve warmly.

Nutritional Information: 270 calories, 13g protein, 35g carbohydrates, 9g fat, 10g fiber, 0mg cholesterol, 200mg sodium, 600mg potassium.

SPAGHETTI SQUASH & TURKEY MEATBALLS

Yield

2 servings

Preparation Time

15 minutes

Cooking Time

40 Minutes

INGREDIENTS

- 1 small spaghetti squash
- 1/2 pound ground turkey
- 1/4 cup grated parmesan cheese
- 1/4 cup breadcrumbs (optional, or use almond flour for grain-free)
- 1 egg
- 1/2 teaspoon garlic powder
- 1/2 teaspoon dried oregano
- 1/2 teaspoon salt
- 1/4 teaspoon black pepper
- 1 cup marinara sauce (store-bought or homemade, low-sugar)
- 1 tablespoon olive oil
- Fresh parsley for garnish (optional)

DIRECTIONS

1. Preheat the oven to 400°F (200°C). Cut the spaghetti squash in half lengthwise, scoop out the seeds, and drizzle the cut sides with olive oil. Place the squash cut side on a baking sheet and roast for 30-40 minutes, or until the flesh quickly shreds into strands with a fork. Once cooked, use a fork to scrape out the "spaghetti" and set aside.

2. Prepare the turkey meatballs. In a medium bowl, mix the ground turkey, parmesan cheese, breadcrumbs (or almond flour), egg, garlic powder, oregano, salt, and pepper until combined. Form the mixture into small meatballs (about 1 inch in diameter).

3. Heat a large skillet over medium heat and add 1 tablespoon olive oil. Add the turkey meatballs and cook for 7-10 minutes, turning occasionally, until browned on all sides and cooked through.

4. Pour the marinara sauce over the cooked meatballs and simmer for 5-7 minutes until the sauce is heated and the flavors meld.

5. Divide the spaghetti squash between two plates, top with the turkey meatballs and marinara sauce, and garnish with fresh parsley, if desired.

Nutritional Information: 390 calories, 28g protein, 27g carbohydrates, 18g fat, 6g fiber, 120mg cholesterol, 720mg sodium, 900mg potassium.

MEDITERRANEAN-INSPIRED WRAPS AND BOWLS

CHICKPEA & CUCUMBER WRAP

Yield
2 servings

Preparation Time
10 minutes

Cooking Time
0 Minutes

INGREDIENTS

- 2 whole wheat tortillas
- 1/2 cup canned chickpeas, drained and rinsed
- 1/2 cup cucumber, diced
- 1/4 cup hummus
- 1 tablespoon olive oil
- 1 tablespoon lemon juice
- 1 tablespoon fresh parsley, chopped
- Salt and pepper to taste

DIRECTIONS

1. Prepare the chickpea mixture. In a small bowl, gently mash the chickpeas with a fork until partially broken down. Drizzle with olive oil and lemon juice and sprinkle with chopped parsley, salt, and pepper. Mix well.
2. Lay the whole wheat tortillas flat and spread 2 tablespoons of hummus on each.
3. Top each tortilla with the chickpea mixture and diced cucumber. Spread the ingredients evenly.
4. Fold in the sides of the tortilla, then roll it up tightly. Slice in half and serve immediately.

Nutritional Information: 310 calories, 9g protein, 35g carbohydrates, 14g fat, 8g fiber, 0mg cholesterol, 370mg sodium, 500mg potassium.

MEDITERRANEAN TUNA SALAD BOWL

INGREDIENTS

- 1 can (5 oz) tuna in water, drained
- 1/2 cup cucumber, diced
- 1/4 cup red onion, finely diced
- 1/4 cup Kalamata olives, sliced
- 1 tablespoon capers (optional)
- 2 tablespoons olive oil
- 1 tablespoon lemon juice
- 1/2 teaspoon dried oregano
- Salt and pepper to taste
- Fresh parsley for garnish (optional)

Yield
2 servings

Preparation Time
10 minutes

Cooking Time
0 Minutes

DIRECTIONS

1. Prepare the salad. In a medium bowl, combine the drained tuna, diced cucumber, red onion, olives, and capers (if using).
2. Make the dressing. Whisk together the olive oil, lemon juice, oregano, salt, and pepper in a small bowl.
3. Pour the dressing over the tuna mixture and gently toss everything to coat evenly.
4. Divide the salad between two bowls and garnish with fresh parsley if desired. Serve immediately.

Nutritional Information: 300 calories, 22g protein, 8g carbohydrates, 21g fat, 2g fiber, 30mg cholesterol, 700mg sodium, 450mg potassium.

FALAFEL & VEGGIE WRAP

Yield
2 servings

Preparation Time
10 minutes

Cooking Time
5 Minutes

INGREDIENTS

- 4 store-bought falafel balls (or homemade)
- 2 whole wheat tortillas
- 1 cup romaine lettuce, chopped
- 1/2 cup cherry tomatoes, halved
- 2 tablespoons tahini
- 1 tablespoon lemon juice
- 1 tablespoon water (to thin the tahini)
- Salt and pepper to taste
- Fresh parsley for garnish (optional)

DIRECTIONS

1. Heat the falafel. Warm the falafel balls in a skillet over medium heat for 3-5 minutes or microwave until heated.
2. Prepare the Tahini Sauce. Whisk together the tahini, lemon juice, water, and a pinch of salt and pepper in a small bowl until smooth. Add more water if needed to reach your desired consistency.
3. Place 2 falafel balls in the center of each tortilla, then top with chopped romaine lettuce and halved cherry tomatoes.
4. Drizzle the creamy tahini sauce over the falafel and veggies. Fold in the sides of the tortilla and roll it up tightly.
5. Slice in half and serve immediately, garnished with fresh parsley if desired.

Nutritional Information: 350 calories, 12g protein, 42g carbohydrates, 15g fat, 8g fiber, 0mg cholesterol, 500mg sodium, 600mg potassium.

CUCUMBER & HUMMUS WRAP

Yield
2 servings

Preparation Time
10 minutes

Cooking Time
0 Minutes

INGREDIENTS

- 2 whole wheat tortillas
- 1/2 cup hummus
- 1 small cucumber, thinly sliced
- 1/2 cup shredded carrots
- 2 tablespoons fresh parsley, chopped
- 1 tablespoon olive oil
- 1 tablespoon lemon juice
- Salt and pepper to taste

DIRECTIONS

1. Lay the whole wheat tortillas flat on a clean surface.
2. Spread 1/4 cup of hummus evenly over each tortilla. Layer the cucumber slices and shredded carrots on top of the hummus.
3. Drizzle olive oil and lemon juice over the veggies. Sprinkle with chopped parsley, salt, and pepper to taste.
4. Fold in the sides of each tortilla and roll it up tightly. Slice in half and serve immediately.

Nutritional Information: 290 calories, 8g protein, 38g carbohydrates, 12g fat, 8g fiber, 0mg cholesterol, 350mg sodium, 500mg potassium.

GREEK CHICKEN BOWL

Yield

2 servings

Preparation Time

10 minutes

Cooking Time

20 minutes

INGREDIENTS

- 1/2 cup quinoa, rinsed
- 1 cup water or chicken broth (for cooking quinoa)
- 1 chicken breast, grilled and sliced
- 1/2 cup cucumber, chopped
- 1/4 cup Kalamata olives, sliced
- 1/4 cup feta cheese, crumbled
- 2 tablespoons olive oil
- 1 tablespoon lemon juice
- 1/2 teaspoon dried oregano
- Salt and pepper to taste
- Fresh parsley for garnish (optional)

DIRECTIONS

1. Cook the quinoa. In a medium saucepan, bring 1 cup of water (or chicken broth) to a boil. Add the quinoa, reduce the heat to low, cover, and simmer for 15 minutes or until the liquid is absorbed and the quinoa is tender. Fluff with a fork and set aside.

2. Grill the Chicken. While the quinoa is cooking, grill the chicken breast on a pan or outdoor grill for 5-7 minutes per side until fully cooked. Slice the chicken into strips.

3. Divide the cooked quinoa between two bowls. Top with sliced grilled chicken, chopped cucumber, Kalamata olives, and crumbled feta cheese.

4. Make the Dressing. In a small bowl, whisk together the olive oil, lemon juice, oregano, salt, and pepper.

5. Drizzle the dressing over the bowls. Garnish with fresh parsley if desired and serve immediately.

Nutritional Information: 430 calories, 30g protein, 24g carbohydrates, 22g fat, 5g fiber, 70mg cholesterol, 600mg sodium, 800mg potassium.

ONE-PAN VEGGIE-PACKED SKILLETS

BELL PEPPER & TURKEY SKILLET

Yield
2 servings

Preparation Time
10 minutes

Cooking Time
15 Minutes

INGREDIENTS

- 1/2 pound ground turkey
- 1 red bell pepper, diced
- 1 yellow bell pepper, diced
- 1/2 onion, diced
- 2 cloves garlic, minced
- 1 tablespoon olive oil
- 1 teaspoon ground cumin
- 1/2 teaspoon smoked paprika (optional)
- Salt and pepper to taste
- Fresh parsley or cilantro for garnish (optional)

DIRECTIONS

1. Heat the olive oil in a large skillet over medium heat. Add the ground turkey and cook for 5-7 minutes, breaking it up with a spatula, until browned and cooked.
2. Add the diced bell peppers, onion, and minced garlic to the skillet with the turkey. Sauté for 5-7 minutes until the vegetables are softened.
3. Sprinkle in the cumin, smoked paprika (if using), salt, and pepper. Stir to coat the turkey and vegetables evenly with the seasonings.
4. Once everything is cooked and well combined, remove from heat. If desired, garnish with fresh parsley or cilantro and serve hot.

Nutritional Information: 310 calories, 25g protein, 12g carbohydrates, 18g fat, 3g fiber, 80mg cholesterol, 450mg sodium, 750mg potassium.

GROUND TURKEY & CARROT HASH

Yield
2 servings

Preparation Time
10 minutes

Cooking Time
15 Minutes

INGREDIENTS

- 1/2 pound ground turkey
- 2 medium carrots, peeled and shredded
- 1/2 onion, diced
- 2 cloves garlic, minced
- 1 tablespoon olive oil
- 1 teaspoon ground cumin
- 1/2 teaspoon smoked paprika (optional)
- Salt and pepper to taste
- Fresh parsley for garnish (optional)

DIRECTIONS

1. Cook the Ground Turkey. Heat olive oil in a large skillet over medium heat. Add the ground turkey and cook for 5-7 minutes, breaking it up with a spatula, until browned and cooked.
2. Add the diced onion and minced garlic to the skillet and sauté for 2-3 minutes until softened. Stir in the shredded carrots and cook for another 5 minutes, stirring occasionally, until the carrots are tender.
3. Sprinkle in the cumin, smoked paprika (if using), salt, and pepper. Stir to combine and cook for 1-2 minutes to let the flavors meld.
4. Remove from heat, garnish with fresh parsley if desired, and serve hot.

Nutritional Information: 300 calories, 25g protein, 12g carbohydrates, 16g fat, 4g fiber, 80mg cholesterol, 450mg sodium, 700mg potassium.

BROCCOLI & CHICKEN SAUSAGE STIR-FRY

Yield
2 servings

Preparation Time
10 minutes

Cooking Time
15 Minutes

INGREDIENTS

- 2 chicken sausages (precooked), sliced
- 2 cups broccoli florets
- 1 bell pepper, diced
- 1/2 onion, diced
- 2 cloves garlic, minced
- 1 tablespoon olive oil
- 1/4 teaspoon red pepper flakes (optional, for spice)
- Salt and pepper to taste
- 1 tablespoon low-sodium soy sauce (optional for extra flavor)

DIRECTIONS

1. Sauté the Chicken Sausage. Heat 1 tablespoon of olive oil in a large skillet over medium heat. Add the sliced chicken sausage and cook for 3-4 minutes, stirring occasionally, until lightly browned.
2. Add the diced onion, garlic, broccoli florets, and bell pepper to the skillet. Cook for 5-7 minutes, stirring occasionally, until the broccoli is tender but still crisp.
3. Sprinkle in the red pepper flakes (if using) and season with salt and pepper. Drizzle with soy sauce for added flavor, then cook for another 1-2 minutes until everything is well combined and heated.
4. Remove from heat and serve hot.

Nutritional Information: 320 calories, 22g protein, 16g carbohydrates, 18g fat, 6g fiber, 60mg cholesterol, 600mg sodium, 800mg potassium.

SWEET POTATO & KALE SKILLET

Yield
2 servings

Preparation Time
20 minutes

Cooking Time
15 Minutes

INGREDIENTS

- 1 medium sweet potato, peeled and diced
- 2 cups kale, stems removed and chopped
- 1/2 onion, diced
- 2 cloves garlic, minced
- 1 tablespoon olive oil
- 1/4 teaspoon smoked paprika (optional)
- Salt and pepper to taste
- 1 tablespoon water (optional, to help steam the kale)
- Fresh parsley for garnish (optional)

DIRECTIONS

1. Cook the Sweet Potatoes. Heat olive oil in a large skillet over medium heat. Add the diced sweet potatoes and cook for 8-10 minutes, stirring occasionally, until they soften and lightly brown.
2. Add the diced onion and minced garlic to the skillet with the sweet potatoes. Sauté for 3-4 minutes until the onions become translucent and fragrant.
3. Stir in the chopped kale and smoked paprika (if using). If the skillet seems dry, add 1 tablespoon of water to help steam the kale. Cook for another 3-5 minutes, stirring occasionally, until the kale is wilted and tender.
4. Season with salt and pepper to taste. If desired, garnish with fresh parsley and serve immediately.

Nutritional Information: 250 calories, 4g protein, 38g carbohydrates, 10g fat, 7g fiber, 0mg cholesterol, 220mg sodium, 750mg potassium.

ZUCCHINI & TOFU STIR-FRY

Yield
2 servings

Preparation Time
10 minutes

Cooking Time
15 Minutes

INGREDIENTS

- 1 block (8 oz) firm tofu, cubed
- 1 medium zucchini, sliced into half-moons
- 1/2 onion, thinly sliced
- 2 cloves garlic, minced
- 2 tablespoons soy sauce (low sodium)
- 1 tablespoon olive oil or sesame oil (for cooking)
- 1/2 teaspoon ground ginger (optional)
- 1/2 teaspoon red pepper flakes (optional, for spice)
- 1 tablespoon green onions, chopped (for garnish)
- 1 tablespoon sesame seeds (optional, for garnish)
- Salt and pepper to taste

DIRECTIONS

1. Prepare the Tofu. In a large skillet, heat 1 tablespoon of oil over medium heat. Add the cubed tofu and cook for 5-7 minutes, turning occasionally, until golden and crispy on all sides. Remove the tofu from the skillet and set aside.

2. Add the sliced zucchini, onion, and garlic in the same skillet. Cook for 5-6 minutes, stirring occasionally, until the zucchini is tender and the onions are translucent.

3. Stir in the soy sauce, ground ginger (if using), and red pepper flakes. Return the cooked tofu to the skillet and toss everything together to coat evenly. Cook for another 2-3 minutes to allow the flavors to meld.

4. Remove from heat and garnish with chopped green onions and sesame seeds. Serve immediately.

Nutritional Information: 280 calories, 14g protein, 16g carbohydrates, 18g fat, 5g fiber, 0mg cholesterol, 600mg sodium, 600mg potassium.

CHAPTER 5

DINNER RECIPES

After a long day, the last thing anyone wants is to spend hours in the kitchen. But don't worry—I've got you covered with these quick and easy dinner ideas! They're designed to be satisfying and simple, helping you quickly put a healthy, diabetes-friendly meal on the table. With minimal prep and straightforward ingredients, you can enjoy a delicious dinner that keeps you on track with your health goals.

Whether cooking for yourself or the whole family, these dinner options make it easy to end your day on a nourishing note.

QUICK AND EASY DINNER IDEAS

1

ONE-POT DINNERS

These simple and satisfying dinners are made in one pot or pan and feature hearty ingredients like chicken, beans, or vegetables for minimal cleanup and maximum flavor.

2

LEAN PROTEIN ENTRÉES

Delicious and balanced dinners using lean proteins like grilled chicken, baked fish, or tofu paired with fresh vegetables for a healthy and filling meal.

3

VEGGIE-FORWARD PLATES

Nutritious and colorful dinners that highlight a variety of vegetables, with options like roasted veggie medleys, stir-fries, and grain bowls for a wholesome, plant-focused meal.

4

LOW-CARB COMFORT CLASSICS

Enjoy comforting dinners with a low-carb twist. Use ingredients like cauliflower, zucchini, and lean proteins to create satisfying, diabetes-friendly meals without the extra carbs.

ONE-POT DINNERS

ONE-POT BEEF & BEAN CHILI

Yield
4 servings

Preparation Time
10 minutes

Cooking Time
30 Minutes

INGREDIENTS

- 1 tablespoon olive oil
- 1 pound lean ground beef
- 1 medium onion, diced
- 2 cloves garlic, minced
- 1 bell pepper, diced (any color)
- 1 can (15 oz) kidney beans, drained and rinsed
- 1 can (14.5 oz) diced tomatoes (with juice)
- 1 can (8 oz) tomato sauce
- 1 tablespoon chili powder
- 1 teaspoon ground cumin
- 1 teaspoon smoked paprika
- 1/2 teaspoon dried oregano
- Salt and pepper to taste
- 1/2 cup water or beef broth (optional, for desired consistency)
- Optional toppings: shredded cheese, sour cream, chopped green onions, or cilantro

DIRECTIONS

1. Cook the Beef. Heat the olive oil in a large pot or Dutch oven over medium heat. Add the ground beef and cook, breaking it up with a spoon, until browned and fully cooked about 5-7 minutes. Drain excess fat if necessary.
2. Add the diced onion, garlic, and bell pepper to the pot with the beef. Sauté for 3-4 minutes until the vegetables are softened.
3. Stir in the kidney beans, diced tomatoes (with their juice), tomato sauce, chili powder, cumin, smoked paprika, and oregano. Season with salt and pepper to taste.
4. Add 1/2 cup of water or beef broth if the chili seems too thick. Bring the mixture to a simmer, reduce the heat to low, and let it cook uncovered for 20-25 minutes, stirring occasionally, until the flavors meld and the chili thickens to your desired consistency.
5. Ladle the chili into bowls and serve hot. Garnish with your choice of toppings, such as shredded cheese, sour cream, chopped green onions, or cilantro.

Nutritional Information: 350 calories, 25g protein, 25g carbohydrates, 15g fat, 8g fiber, 60mg cholesterol, 700mg sodium, 800mg potassium.

LEMON GARLIC SHRIMP & ASPARAGUS

Yield
2 servings

Preparation Time
10 minutes

Cooking Time
15 Minutes

INGREDIENTS

- 1 tablespoon olive oil
- 1/2 pound large shrimp, raw, peeled, and deveined
- 1 bunch asparagus, trimmed and cut into 2-inch pieces
- 2 cloves garlic, minced
- Zest and juice of 1 lemon
- 1/4 teaspoon red pepper flakes (optional, for a bit of heat)
- Salt and pepper to taste
- Fresh parsley, chopped (for garnish)

DIRECTIONS

1. Prepare the Shrimp. Pat the raw, peeled, and deveined shrimp dry with paper towels, then season with salt and pepper.
2. Cook the Asparagus. Heat the olive oil in a large skillet over medium heat. Add the asparagus and sauté for 3-4 minutes until it softens but remains crisp-tender. Remove the asparagus from the skillet and set aside.
3. Add the shrimp to the same skillet and cook for 2-3 minutes on each side until they are pink and opaque. Remove the shrimp from the skillet and set aside with the asparagus.
4. Make the Lemon-Garlic Sauce. In the same skillet, add the minced garlic and sauté for about 30 seconds until fragrant. Add the lemon zest, lemon juice, and red pepper flakes (if using), stirring to combine. Let the sauce simmer for 1 minute.
5. Return the shrimp and asparagus to the skillet, tossing them in the lemon-garlic sauce until well coated and heated. Serve immediately, garnished with chopped fresh parsley.

Nutritional Information: 210 calories, 24g protein, 10g carbohydrates, 9g fat, 4g fiber, 220mg cholesterol, 450mg sodium, 500mg potassium.

MEDITERRANEAN CHICKEN & QUINOA

INGREDIENTS

- 1 tablespoon olive oil
- 4 boneless, skinless chicken thighs
- Salt and pepper to taste
- 1 teaspoon dried oregano
- 1 cup quinoa, rinsed
- 2 cups low-sodium chicken broth
- 1/2 cup pitted Kalamata olives, halved
- 1 cup cherry tomatoes, halved
- 2 cups fresh spinach, roughly chopped
- 2 cloves garlic, minced
- Juice of 1 lemon
- Fresh parsley, chopped (for garnish)

Yield
4 servings

Preparation Time
10 minutes

Cooking Time
35 Minutes

DIRECTIONS

1. Season the Chicken: Rub chicken thighs with salt, pepper, and oregano.
2. Cook the Chicken: Heat olive oil in a pot over medium heat and cook chicken thighs for 5-6 minutes per side until golden and cooked through. Remove and set aside.
3. Cook the Quinoa: In the same pot, sauté garlic for 1 minute. Add quinoa and chicken broth, bring to a boil, then cover and simmer for 15 minutes.
4. Combine Ingredients: Stir in olives, tomatoes, and spinach. Return chicken to the pot, cover, and cook for another 5-10 minutes until quinoa is tender.
5. Finish and Serve: Drizzle lemon juice over the dish, garnish with parsley, and serve.

Nutritional Information: 400 calories, 28g protein, 28g carbohydrates, 20g fat, 5g fiber, 80mg cholesterol, 600mg sodium, 750mg potassium.

VEGGIE-LOADED ONE-POT PASTA

INGREDIENTS

- 1 tablespoon olive oil
- 1 small onion, diced
- 2 cloves garlic, minced
- 8 oz mushrooms, sliced
- 1 can (14.5 oz) diced tomatoes (with juice)
- 4 cups low-sodium vegetable broth
- 8 oz whole wheat pasta (such as penne or rotini)
- 4 cups fresh spinach, roughly chopped
- 1 teaspoon dried basil
- 1 teaspoon dried oregano
- Salt and pepper to taste
- 1/4 cup grated Parmesan cheese (optional for serving)
- Fresh basil leaves for garnish (optional)

Yield
4 servings

Preparation Time
10 minutes

Cooking Time
20 Minutes

DIRECTIONS

1. Heat the olive oil over medium heat in a large pot. Add the diced onion and cook until softened about 3-4 minutes. Add the garlic and sliced mushrooms, and sauté for another 3-4 minutes until the mushrooms are tender.
2. Pour in the diced tomatoes (with their juice) and vegetable broth. Stir in the dried basil, dried oregano, salt, and pepper.
3. Cook the Pasta. Add the whole wheat pasta to the pot, stirring to combine. Bring the mixture to a boil, then reduce the heat to medium-low. Cover and simmer for 10-12 minutes, stirring occasionally, until the pasta is al dente.
4. Stir in the chopped spinach and cook for 2-3 minutes until the spinach is wilted and fully incorporated.
5. Divide the pasta among bowls and, if desired, sprinkle with grated Parmesan cheese and garnish with fresh basil leaves. Serve hot.

Nutritional Information: 320 calories, 10g protein, 50g carbohydrates, 8g fat, 8g fiber, 5mg cholesterol, 500mg sodium, 700mg potassium.

CHICKEN & VEGETABLE SKILLET

INGREDIENTS

- 2 boneless, skinless chicken breasts
- 1 tablespoon olive oil
- 1 small zucchini, sliced into rounds
- 1 bell pepper, sliced into strips (any color)
- 1 cup cherry tomatoes, halved
- 2 cloves garlic, minced
- 1 teaspoon dried Italian seasoning
- Salt and pepper to taste
- Fresh basil leaves, for garnish (optional)

Yield
2 servings

Preparation Time
10 minutes

Cooking Time
20 Minutes

DIRECTIONS

1. Prepare the Chicken. Season the chicken breasts (whole or sliced into strips) with salt, pepper, and half of the dried Italian seasoning.
2. Heat the olive oil in a large skillet over medium heat. Add the chicken breasts and cook for 6-7 minutes on each side (or 3-4 minutes per side if sliced), until golden brown and cooked through. Remove the chicken from the skillet and set aside.
3. In the same skillet, add the garlic and cook for 1 minute until fragrant. Add the zucchini, bell pepper, and cherry tomatoes. Season with the remaining Italian seasoning, salt, and pepper. Cook for 5-7 minutes, stirring occasionally, until the vegetables are tender.
4. Return the chicken to the skillet, nestling it among the vegetables. Cook for an additional 2 minutes to heat the chicken through. Garnish with fresh basil leaves if desired and serve hot.

Nutritional Information: 320 calories, 30g protein, 12g carbohydrates, 15g fat, 3g fiber, 75mg cholesterol, 360mg sodium, 850mg potassium.

LEAN PROTEIN ENTRÉES

TURKEY MEATLOAF WITH ROASTED BRUSSELS SPROUTS

Yield
4 servings

Preparation Time
15 minutes

Cooking Time
45 minutes

INGREDIENTS

For the Turkey Meatloaf:

- 1 lb lean ground turkey
- 1/2 cup whole wheat breadcrumbs
- 1 egg, lightly beaten
- 1 small onion, finely diced
- 2 cloves garlic, minced
- 1 tablespoon Worcestershire sauce
- 1 tablespoon tomato paste
- 1 teaspoon dried thyme
- 1 teaspoon dried oregano
- Salt and pepper to taste

For the Roasted Brussels Sprouts:

- 1 lb Brussels sprouts, trimmed and halved
- 1 tablespoon olive oil
- 1 teaspoon balsamic vinegar
- Salt and pepper to taste

DIRECTIONS

1. Preheat oven to 375°F (190°C).

2. Prepare the Meatloaf: In a bowl, mix ground turkey, breadcrumbs, egg, onion, garlic, Worcestershire sauce, tomato paste, thyme, oregano, salt, and pepper. Shape into a loaf and place in a greased pan or on a parchment-lined sheet. Bake for 35-40 minutes until the internal temperature reaches 165°F.

3. Roast the Brussels Sprouts: While the meatloaf bakes, toss Brussels sprouts with olive oil, balsamic vinegar, salt, and pepper. Spread on a baking sheet and roast for 20-25 minutes, turning halfway through.

4. Serve: Slice the meatloaf and serve with the roasted Brussels sprouts.

Nutritional Information: 350 calories, 28g protein, 20g carbohydrates, 16g fat, 5g fiber, 120mg cholesterol, 480mg sodium, 800mg potassium.

TOFU STIR-FRY WITH SNOW PEAS AND CARROTS

INGREDIENTS

- 8 oz firm tofu, pressed and cubed
- 1 tablespoon sesame oil (or olive oil)
- 2 cloves garlic, minced
- 1 tablespoon fresh ginger, minced
- 1 cup snow peas, trimmed
- 1 large carrot, julienned or thinly sliced
- 2 tablespoons low-sodium soy sauce
- 1 tablespoon rice vinegar
- 1 tablespoon sugar-free teriyaki sauce (or tamari for a less sweet option)
- 1 teaspoon sesame seeds (optional, for garnish)
- 2 green onions, sliced (optional, for garnish)

Yield
2 servings

Preparation Time
10 minutes

Cooking Time
15 Minutes

DIRECTIONS

1. Prepare the Tofu. After pressing the tofu to remove excess moisture, cut it into bite-sized cubes. Heat the sesame oil in a large skillet or wok over medium-high heat. Add the tofu cubes and cook for about 5-7 minutes, turning occasionally, until golden brown on all sides. Remove the tofu from the skillet and set aside.

2. In the same skillet, add the minced garlic and ginger. Sauté for about 1 minute until fragrant. Add the snow peas and julienned carrots, and stir-fry for 3-4 minutes until the vegetables are tender-crisp.

3. Return the tofu to the skillet. Add the soy sauce, rice vinegar, and sugar-free teriyaki sauce or tamari. Stir everything together and cook for 2-3 minutes, allowing the tofu to absorb the flavors and the sauce to thicken slightly.

4. Divide the stir-fry between plates or bowls. If desired, garnish with sesame seeds and sliced green onions. Serve hot, with or without a side of steamed rice.

Nutritional Information: 270 calories, 15g protein, 12g carbohydrates, 18g fat, 4g fiber, 0mg cholesterol, 550mg sodium, 450mg potassium.

GRILLED LEMON HERB CHICKEN WITH STEAMED BROCCOLI

Yield
2 servings

Preparation Time
10 minutes (plus marinating time)

Cooking Time
15 Minutes

INGREDIENTS

- 2 boneless, skinless chicken breasts
- 2 tablespoons olive oil
- Juice of 1 lemon
- Zest of 1 lemon
- 2 cloves garlic, minced
- 1 teaspoon dried oregano
- 1 teaspoon dried thyme
- Salt and pepper to taste
- 1 small head of broccoli, cut into florets

DIRECTIONS

1. Mix olive oil, lemon juice, zest, garlic, oregano, thyme, salt, and pepper. Marinate chicken in the mixture for at least 30 minutes in the fridge.

2. Grill the Chicken. Preheat the grill to medium-high. Grill chicken for 6-7 minutes per side until cooked at 165°F (74°C). Let rest before serving.

3. Steam the Broccoli. While grilling, steam broccoli for 5-7 minutes until tender crisp.

4. Plate the grilled chicken with steamed broccoli. Garnish with lemon zest if desired.

Nutritional Information: 320 calories, 35g protein, 8g carbohydrates, 16g fat, 4g fiber, 75mg cholesterol, 180mg sodium, 650mg potassium.

HERB-CRUSTED COD WITH SAUTÉED SPINACH

INGREDIENTS

For the Herb-Crusted Cod:

- 2 cod fillets (about 6 oz each)
- 1/2 cup whole wheat breadcrumbs
- 1 tablespoon fresh parsley, finely chopped
- 1 tablespoon fresh thyme leaves, finely chopped
- 1 teaspoon lemon zest
- 1 clove garlic, minced
- 2 tablespoons olive oil (divided)
- Salt and pepper to taste

For the Sautéed Spinach:

- 1 tablespoon olive oil
- 2 cloves garlic, thinly sliced
- 4 cups fresh spinach leaves
- Salt and pepper to taste
- Juice of 1/2 lemon (optional, for finishing)

Yield
2 servings

Preparation Time
10 minutes

Cooking Time
15 Minutes

DIRECTIONS

1. Preheat the oven to 400°F (200°C).
2. Prepare the Herb Crust. Mix breadcrumbs, parsley, thyme, lemon zest, garlic, salt, pepper, and 1 tablespoon of olive oil in a bowl.
3. Crust the Cod. Pat cod fillets dry, season with salt and pepper, and place on an oiled, foil-lined baking sheet. Press the herb mixture onto each fillet, drizzle with olive oil, and bake for 10-12 minutes until cooked through and golden.
4. Sauté the Spinach. Heat 1 tablespoon olive oil in a skillet, sauté garlic for 1 minute, then add spinach and cook until wilted (2-3 minutes). Season with salt, pepper, and lemon juice if desired.
5. Plate the cod with the sautéed spinach and enjoy!

Nutritional Information: 350 calories, 30g protein, 15g carbohydrates, 18g fat, 5g fiber, 70mg cholesterol, 400mg sodium, 900mg potassium.

BAKED SALMON WITH GARLIC ASPARAGUS

Yield
2 servings

Preparation Time
10 minutes

Cooking Time
15 Minutes

INGREDIENTS

- 2 salmon fillets (about 6 oz each)
- 1 tablespoon olive oil
- 2 cloves garlic, minced
- Juice of 1/2 lemon
- Zest of 1/2 lemon
- 1 bunch asparagus, trimmed
- Salt and pepper to taste
- Fresh parsley, chopped (for garnish)

DIRECTIONS

1. Preheat your oven to 400°F (200°C).
2. Prepare the Salmon. Place the salmon fillets on a baking sheet lined with parchment paper or lightly greased. Drizzle with 1/2 tablespoon of olive oil, then season with salt, pepper, minced garlic, lemon juice, and lemon zest.
3. Prepare the Asparagus. Toss the asparagus spears with the remaining 1/2 tablespoon of olive oil, minced garlic, salt, and pepper. Arrange the asparagus around the salmon on the baking sheet.
4. Place the baking sheet in the preheated oven and bake for 12-15 minutes until the salmon is cooked and flakes easily with a fork, and the asparagus is tender-crisp.
5. Remove the salmon and asparagus from the oven and transfer them to plates. Garnish with chopped fresh parsley and additional lemon wedges, if desired. Serve immediately.

Nutritional Information: 350 calories, 30g protein, 10g carbohydrates, 20g fat, 4g fiber, 70mg cholesterol, 180mg sodium, 800mg potassium.

VEGGIE-FORWARD PLATES

CAULIFLOWER RICE & VEGGIE STIR-FRY

Yield

2 servings

Preparation Time

10 minutes

Cooking Time

15 Minutes

INGREDIENTS

- 2 cups cauliflower rice (store-bought or homemade)
- 1 tablespoon sesame oil (or olive oil)
- 1 medium carrot, julienned or thinly sliced
- 1/2 cup bell peppers, thinly sliced (any color)
- 1/2 cup green peas (fresh or frozen)
- 2 cloves garlic, minced
- 1 teaspoon fresh ginger, minced
- 2 tablespoons low-sodium soy sauce (or tamari for gluten-free)
- 1 tablespoon rice vinegar
- 1 teaspoon sesame seeds (optional, for garnish)
- 2 green onions, sliced (optional, for garnish)

DIRECTIONS

1. Prepare the Cauliflower Rice. Cut a whole cauliflower into florets and pulse in a food processor until it resembles rice. Measure out 2 cups and set aside.

2. Sauté the Vegetables. Heat the sesame oil over medium-high heat in a large skillet or wok. Add the minced garlic and fresh ginger, sautéing for about 1 minute until fragrant. Add the carrots and bell peppers, and stir-fry for 3-4 minutes until they begin to soften.

3. Stir in the cauliflower rice and green peas. Cook for another 3-4 minutes, stirring frequently, until the cauliflower rice is tender but not mushy.

4. In a small bowl, whisk together the soy sauce and rice vinegar. Pour the sauce over the stir-fry, tossing to coat the vegetables evenly. Cook for an additional 2 minutes to allow the flavors to meld.

5. Transfer the stir-fry to plates or bowls. If desired, garnish with sesame seeds and sliced green onions. Serve hot for a quick, low-carb dinner.

Nutritional Information: 200 calories, 5g protein, 20g carbohydrates, 10g fat, 6g fiber, 0mg cholesterol, 500mg sodium, 450mg potassium.

STIR-FRIED BROCCOLI & TOFU WITH SESAME SAUCE

INGREDIENTS

- 8 oz firm tofu, pressed and cubed
- 1 tablespoon sesame oil (or olive oil)
- 2 cups broccoli florets
- 1/2 red bell pepper, sliced
- 2 cloves garlic, minced
- 1 tablespoon soy sauce (low sodium)
- 1 tablespoon rice vinegar
- 1 tablespoon sesame seeds
- 1 teaspoon fresh ginger, minced
- 1 teaspoon honey or maple syrup (optional, for sweetness)
- 2 green onions, sliced (optional, for garnish)

Yield
2 servings

Preparation Time
10 minutes

Cooking Time
15 Minutes

DIRECTIONS

1. Cook the Tofu. Cut pressed tofu into cubes and sauté in sesame oil over medium-high heat for 5-7 minutes until golden. Set aside.
2. In the same skillet, cook garlic and ginger for 1 minute. Add broccoli and red bell pepper, and stir-fry for 3-4 minutes until tender-crisp.
3. Make the Sauce. Whisk soy sauce, rice vinegar, and honey or maple syrup (if using) in a small bowl. Pour over the veggies.
4. Add tofu back to the skillet and toss everything to combine. Cook for 2-3 more minutes.
5. Garnish with sesame seeds and green onions if desired. Serve hot.

Nutritional Information: 290 calories, 15g protein, 16g carbohydrates, 18g fat, 6g fiber, 0mg cholesterol, 470mg sodium, 480mg potassium.

ROASTED VEGGIE MEDLEY WITH BALSAMIC GLAZE

Yield
2 servings

Preparation Time
10 minutes

Cooking Time
15 Minutes

INGREDIENTS

- 1 red bell pepper, cut into 1-inch pieces
- 1 yellow bell pepper, cut into 1-inch pieces
- 1 zucchini, sliced into rounds
- 1 red onion, cut into wedges
- 1 cup cherry tomatoes
- 2 tablespoons olive oil
- Salt and pepper to taste
- 2 tablespoons balsamic vinegar
- 1 tablespoon honey or maple syrup (optional, for sweetness)
- Fresh basil leaves for garnish (optional)

DIRECTIONS

1. Preheat the Oven. Preheat your oven to 400°F (200°C).
2. Prepare the Vegetables. Toss the bell peppers, zucchini, red onion, and cherry tomatoes with olive oil, salt, and pepper until evenly coated in a large bowl.
3. Roast the Vegetables. Spread the vegetables in a single layer on a baking sheet lined with parchment paper. Roast in the oven for 20-25 minutes, stirring halfway through, until the vegetables are tender and slightly caramelized.
4. Make the Balsamic Glaze. While the vegetables are roasting, prepare the balsamic glaze. In a small saucepan, combine the balsamic vinegar and honey or maple syrup (if using). Bring to a simmer over medium heat, then reduce the heat to low and let it simmer for 5-7 minutes until the mixture has thickened slightly.
5. Once the vegetables are done roasting, transfer them to a serving platter. Drizzle the balsamic glaze over the top and garnish with fresh basil leaves, if desired. Serve warmly.

Nutritional Information: 120 calories, 2g protein, 15g carbohydrates, 7g fat, 3g fiber, 0mg cholesterol, 180mg sodium, 450mg potassium.

SWEET POTATO & BLACK BEAN GRAIN BOWL

Yield
2 servings

Preparation Time
10 minutes

Cooking Time
25 Minutes

INGREDIENTS

- 1 large sweet potato, peeled and cubed
- 1 tablespoon olive oil
- Salt and pepper to taste
- 1/2 cup quinoa, rinsed
- 1 cup water or low-sodium vegetable broth
- 1 cup black beans, drained and rinsed
- 1 avocado, sliced
- Juice of 1 lime
- Fresh cilantro, chopped (for garnish)
- 2 tablespoons crumbled feta cheese (optional)

DIRECTIONS

1. Roast the Sweet Potatoes. Preheat your oven to 400°F (200°C). Toss the cubed sweet potatoes with olive oil, salt, and pepper. Spread them in a single layer on a baking sheet lined with parchment paper. Roast for 20-25 minutes, or until the sweet potatoes are tender and slightly caramelized, stirring halfway through.

2. Cook the Quinoa. While the sweet potatoes are roasting, cook the quinoa using water or low-sodium vegetable broth according to the package instructions. Once cooked, fluff the quinoa with a fork and set aside.

3. Assemble the Grain Bowls. Divide the cooked quinoa between two bowls. Top each bowl with the roasted sweet potatoes, black beans, and sliced avocado.

4. Finish and Serve: Squeeze the juice of half a lime over each bowl, then sprinkle with fresh cilantro. Add a tablespoon of crumbled feta cheese to each bowl for extra flavor. Serve immediately.

Nutritional Information: 450 calories, 12g protein, 60g carbohydrates, 18g fat, 15g fiber, 0mg cholesterol, 300mg sodium, 900mg potassium.

MEDITERRANEAN STUFFED PEPPERS

INGREDIENTS

- 4 large bell peppers (any color)
- 1/2 cup quinoa, rinsed
- 1 cup water or low-sodium vegetable broth (or according to package instructions)
- 1 tablespoon olive oil
- 2 cups fresh spinach, chopped
- 1/2 cup Kalamata olives, pitted and chopped
- 1/2 cup crumbled feta cheese
- 1 small red onion, finely diced
- 2 cloves garlic, minced
- 1 teaspoon dried oregano
- Salt and pepper to taste
- 2 tablespoons fresh parsley, chopped (optional, for garnish)

Yield
4 servings

Preparation Time
15 minutes

Cooking Time
30 Minutes

DIRECTIONS

1. Preheat the oven to 375°F (190°C). Cut the bell peppers in half, remove the seeds, and brush with olive oil. Place it in a baking dish.

2. Cook quinoa per package instructions. Fluff and set aside.

3. Prepare Filling. Sauté onion and garlic in olive oil for 2-3 minutes. Add spinach until wilted, then stir in quinoa, olives, feta, oregano, salt, and pepper.

4. Stuff Peppers. Fill each pepper with the quinoa mixture. Bake for 25-30 minutes until peppers are tender.

5. Garnish with parsley and serve warm.

Nutritional Information: 280 calories, 8g protein, 30g carbohydrates, 14g fat, 6g fiber, 15mg cholesterol, 550mg sodium, 600mg potassium.

LOW-CARB COMFORT CLASSICS

ZUCCHINI LASAGNA ROLLS

Yield
4 servings

Preparation Time
20 minutes

Cooking Time
30 Minutes

INGREDIENTS

- 2 large zucchinis
- 1 cup ricotta cheese
- 1 cup fresh spinach, chopped
- 1/2 cup grated Parmesan cheese
- 1 egg
- 1 teaspoon dried Italian seasoning
- 1 1/2 cups marinara sauce (store-bought or homemade)
- 1/2 cup shredded mozzarella cheese
- Salt and pepper to taste
- Fresh basil or parsley for garnish (optional)

DIRECTIONS

1. Prepare the Zucchini. Preheat your oven to 375°F (190°C). Use a vegetable peeler or mandolin to slice the zucchinis lengthwise into thin strips. Lightly salt the zucchini slices and set them aside on a paper towel to remove excess moisture.
2. Make the Filling. Combine the ricotta cheese, chopped spinach, Parmesan cheese, egg, Italian seasoning, salt, and pepper in a medium bowl. Mix until well combined.
3. Spread a thin layer of marinara sauce on the bottom of a baking dish. Take each zucchini slice, spread a spoonful of the ricotta mixture onto it, and roll it up tightly. Place each roll seam-side down in the baking dish. Repeat until all the zucchini slices are filled and rolled.
4. Pour the remaining marinara sauce over the zucchini rolls, ensuring they are evenly coated. Sprinkle the shredded mozzarella cheese on top. Bake in the preheated oven for 25-30 minutes or until the cheese is melted and bubbly and the zucchini is tender.
5. Garnish with fresh basil or parsley if desired. Serve warm and enjoy this light, comforting lasagna alternative.

Nutritional Information: 290 calories, 15g protein, 12g carbohydrates, 18g fat, 3g fiber, 85mg cholesterol, 500mg sodium, 550mg potassium.

SPAGHETTI SQUASH ALFREDO

Yield
4 servings

Preparation Time
10 minutes

Cooking Time
40 Minutes

INGREDIENTS

- 1 large spaghetti squash
- 2 tablespoons olive oil, divided
- Salt and pepper to taste
- 2 cloves garlic, minced
- 1 cup heavy cream
- 1/2 cup grated Parmesan cheese
- 1/4 teaspoon nutmeg (optional)
- 1/4 teaspoon red pepper flakes (optional)
- Fresh parsley, chopped (optional, for garnish)

DIRECTIONS

1. Roast the Spaghetti Squash. Preheat oven to 400°F (200°C). Cut the spaghetti squash in half lengthwise and scoop out the seeds. Drizzle the inside of each half with 1 tablespoon of olive oil and season with salt and pepper. Place the squash halves cut side down on a baking sheet lined with parchment paper. Roast for 35-40 minutes or until the flesh is tender and easily shredded with a fork.

2. Make Alfredo Sauce. While the squash is roasting, heat the remaining 1 tablespoon of olive oil in a medium saucepan over medium heat. Add the minced garlic and sauté for 1-2 minutes until fragrant. Stir in the heavy cream and bring to a gentle simmer. Reduce the heat to low and whisk in the Parmesan cheese until the sauce is smooth and creamy. If desired, add nutmeg and red pepper flakes for extra flavor. Season with salt and pepper to taste.

3. Prepare Spaghetti Squash. Once the spaghetti squash is cooked, remove it from the oven and allow it to cool slightly. Use a fork to scrape the flesh into long, spaghetti-like strands. Transfer the strands to a large mixing bowl.

4. Pour the Alfredo sauce over the spaghetti squash strands and toss to coat evenly. Divide the Alfredo-coated squash among plates or bowls. Garnish with fresh parsley if desired, and serve warm.

Nutritional Information: 310 calories, 6g protein, 20g carbohydrates, 24g fat, 4g fiber, 60mg cholesterol, 350mg sodium, 450mg potassium.

CHEESY CAULIFLOWER AND BROCCOLI BAKE

Yield

4 servings

Preparation Time

15 minutes

Cooking Time

30 Minutes

INGREDIENTS

- 1 small head of cauliflower, cut into florets
- 1 small head of broccoli, cut into florets
- 2 tablespoons olive oil
- Salt and pepper to taste
- 1 cup heavy cream
- 1 cup shredded cheddar cheese
- 1/2 cup grated Parmesan cheese
- 1 teaspoon garlic powder
- 1/2 teaspoon mustard powder (optional)
- 1/4 teaspoon paprika (optional, for garnish)
- Fresh parsley, chopped (optional, for garnish)

DIRECTIONS

1. Preheat to 375°F (190°C) and grease a baking dish.
2. Roast Veggies. Toss cauliflower and broccoli with olive oil, salt, and pepper. Spread on a baking sheet lined with parchment paper and roast for 15 minutes until tender.
3. Make Cheese Sauce. While the vegetables are roasting, heat the heavy cream in a medium saucepan over medium heat. Once warm, stir in the shredded cheddar cheese, grated Parmesan cheese, garlic powder, and mustard powder (if using). Stir continuously until the cheese is fully melted and the sauce is smooth and creamy. Season with salt and pepper to taste.
4. Transfer the roasted veggies to the baking dish, pour the cheese sauce over them, and sprinkle with paprika. Bake for 15 minutes or until the top is bubbly and golden. Remove from the oven and let cool slightly before serving. Garnish with chopped fresh parsley, if desired.

Nutritional Information: 310 calories, 10g protein, 12g carbohydrates, 25g fat, 4g fiber, 70mg cholesterol, 450mg sodium, 600mg potassium.

CHICKEN PARMESAN WITH EGGPLANT NOODLES

Yield

4 servings

Preparation Time

20 minutes

Cooking Time

30 minutes

INGREDIENTS

- 2 large eggplants
- 2 boneless, skinless chicken breasts
- 1/2 cup almond flour
- 1/2 cup grated Parmesan cheese
- 1 teaspoon dried Italian seasoning
- 1/2 teaspoon garlic powder
- Salt and pepper to taste
- 1 egg, beaten
- 1 cup marinara sauce (store-bought or homemade)
- 1/2 cup shredded mozzarella cheese
- 2 tablespoons olive oil
- Fresh basil or parsley for garnish (optional)

DIRECTIONS

1. Prepare Eggplant Noodles. Preheat oven to 375°F (190°C). Slice eggplants into thin strips. Lay on a parchment-lined sheet, salt, and sit for 10 minutes. Pat dry.

2. Bread the Chicken. Mix almond flour, Parmesan, Italian seasoning, garlic powder, salt, and pepper. Dip chicken in beaten egg, then coat in the flour mixture.

3. Cook the Chicken. Heat 1 tablespoon olive oil in an oven-safe skillet. Cook the chicken for 3-4 minutes per side until golden. Keep the chicken in the skillet.

4. Top the chicken with marinara sauce and mozzarella. Bake for 15-20 minutes until the cheese is melted and the chicken is cooked through.

5. Cook Eggplant Noodles. While chicken bakes, sauté eggplant in 1 tablespoon olive oil for 3-4 minutes until tender.

6. Plate eggplant noodles, top with chicken, and garnish with basil or parsley.

Nutritional Information: 350 calories, 30g protein, 15g carbohydrates, 20g fat, 7g fiber, 85mg cholesterol, 600mg sodium, 700mg potassium.

CAULIFLOWER MASH SHEPHERD'S PIE

Yield
4 servings

Preparation Time
15 minutes

Cooking Time
30 Minutes

INGREDIENTS

- 1 medium head of cauliflower, cut into florets
- 1 tablespoon olive oil
- 1 lb. ground turkey
- 1 small onion, diced
- 2 cloves garlic, minced
- 1 cup mixed vegetables (frozen peas, carrots, and corn)
- 1/2 cup low-sodium chicken broth
- 1 tablespoon tomato paste
- 1 teaspoon dried thyme
- Salt and pepper to taste
- 1/4 cup grated Parmesan cheese (optional for topping)

DIRECTIONS

1. Prepare the Cauliflower Mash. Boil cauliflower for 10 minutes or until tender. Drain well and transfer to a food processor. Blend until smooth, adding a bit of salt and pepper to taste. Set aside.

2. Cook the Turkey Filling. In a large skillet, heat the olive oil over medium heat. Add the diced onion and garlic and sauté until softened, about 3 minutes. Add the ground turkey and cook until browned, breaking it up with a spoon as it cooks.

3. Add Vegetables and Seasoning. Stir in the mixed vegetables, chicken broth, tomato paste, dried thyme, salt, and pepper. Cook for an additional 5 minutes, allowing the flavors to meld and the mixture to thicken slightly.

4. Preheat your oven to 375°F (190°C). Spread the turkey and vegetable mixture evenly in a baking dish. Top with the cauliflower mash, spreading it out evenly over the filling. If desired, sprinkle with grated Parmesan cheese.

5. Bake in the oven for 20 minutes or until the top is lightly golden. Remove from the oven and let cool slightly before serving.

Nutritional Information: 280 calories, 25g protein, 15g carbohydrates, 12g fat, 5g fiber, 70mg cholesterol, 380mg sodium, 600mg potassium.

CHAPTER 6

SNACK AND APPETIZER RECIPES

Snacks and appetizers can be satisfying and healthy without being complicated. Whether you need a quick bite between meals or something to serve before dinner, these easy-to-make snacks and appetizers are designed to keep your energy up and your blood sugar stable. With simple ingredients and minimal prep time, you can enjoy a variety of tasty, nutritious options that fit perfectly into your diabetes management plan. From crunchy veggie dips to protein-packed bites, these recipes make snacking delicious and effortless.

QUICK AND EASY SNACK AND APPETIZER IDEAS

1 VEGGIE DIPS AND SPREADS

Budget-friendly dips with ingredients like hummus, yogurt, or cottage cheese are served with raw veggies like carrots, cucumbers, and celery.

2 QUICK PROTEIN BITES

These easy snacks use simple ingredients like boiled eggs, peanut butter, and canned tuna to create quick protein-packed bites and energy snacks.

3 AFFORDABLE LOW-CARB SNACK

Creative, low-carb options using staples like cheese, nuts, and roasted chickpeas or simple cucumber and turkey roll-ups.

4 BAKED VEGGIE CHIPS AND FRIES

These homemade alternatives to store-bought snacks, such as baked sweet potato fries, zucchini chips, or kale chips, are all made with affordable ingredients.

VEGGIE DIPS AND SPREADS

AVOCADO YOGURT DIP

Yield
2 servings

Preparation Time
5 minutes

Cooking Time
0 Minutes

INGREDIENTS

- 1 ripe avocado
- 1/4 cup plain Greek yogurt
- 1 tablespoon lime juice
- 1/2 clove garlic, minced
- Salt and pepper to taste
- Raw veggies for dipping: cucumber slices, radishes, celery sticks

DIRECTIONS

1. Prepare the dip. In a small bowl, mash the avocado until smooth. Stir in the Greek yogurt, lime juice, minced garlic, salt, and pepper. Mix until fully combined and creamy.
2. Transfer to a serving bowl and serve with cucumber slices, radishes, and celery sticks.

Nutritional Information: 130 calories, 4g protein, 10g carbohydrates, 9g fat, 5g fiber, 0mg cholesterol, 150mg sodium, 400mg potassium.

GREEK YOGURT TZATZIKI

Yield
2 servings

Preparation Time
10 minutes

Cooking Time
0 Minutes

INGREDIENTS

- 1/2 cup plain Greek yogurt
- 1/4 cucumber, grated and drained
- 1/2 clove garlic, minced
- 1/2 tablespoon olive oil
- 1/2 tablespoon lemon juice
- 1/2 tablespoon fresh dill, chopped (or 1/2 teaspoon dried dill)
- Salt and pepper to taste
- Raw veggies for dipping: bell peppers, cucumber slices, celery sticks

DIRECTIONS

1. Prepare the Tzatziki. In a small bowl, combine the Greek yogurt, grated cucumber (squeeze out excess water), garlic, olive oil, lemon juice, dill, salt, and pepper. Stir well until all ingredients are combined.
2. Transfer to a serving bowl and serve with crunchy raw veggies like bell pepper slices, cucumber slices, and celery sticks.

Nutritional Information: 80 calories, 4g protein, 5g carbohydrates, 5g fat, 1g fiber, 0mg cholesterol, 150mg sodium, 150mg potassium.

COTTAGE CHEESE & HERB SPREAD

Yield
2 servings

Preparation Time
5 minutes

Cooking Time
0 Minutes

INGREDIENTS

- 1/2 cup cottage cheese (low-fat or regular)
- 1/2 tablespoon fresh parsley, chopped
- 1/2 tablespoon fresh chives, chopped
- 1/2 teaspoon lemon juice
- Salt and pepper to taste

Raw veggies for dipping: cherry tomatoes, carrot sticks, celery sticks

DIRECTIONS

1. Prepare the spread. Combine the cottage cheese, parsley, chives, lemon juice, salt, and pepper in a small bowl. Stir until well mixed.
2. Transfer to a serving bowl and serve with cherry tomatoes, carrot sticks, and celery sticks for dipping.

Nutritional Information: 90 calories, 11g protein, 4g carbohydrates, 3g fat, 0g fiber, 10mg cholesterol, 300mg sodium, 200mg potassium.

CLASSIC HUMMUS DIP

Yield
2 servings

Preparation Time
10 minutes

Cooking Time
0 Minutes

INGREDIENTS

- 1/2 can (7.5 oz) chickpeas, drained and rinsed
- 1 tablespoon tahini
- 1 tablespoon olive oil
- 1 tablespoon lemon juice
- 1/2 clove garlic, minced
- 1/4 teaspoon cumin
- Salt and pepper to taste
- 1 tablespoon water (optional for thinning)

Raw veggies for dipping: carrots, cucumbers, celery sticks

DIRECTIONS

1. Blend the Hummus. In a food processor, combine chickpeas, tahini, olive oil, lemon juice, garlic, cumin, salt, and pepper. Blend until smooth.
2. Adjust texture. If the hummus is too thick, add 1 teaspoon of water until it reaches the desired consistency.
3. Transfer to a serving bowl and serve with raw veggies like carrot sticks, cucumber slices, and celery sticks.

Nutritional Information: 90 calories, 3g protein, 8g carbohydrates, 4.5g fat, 2g fiber, 0mg cholesterol, 110mg sodium, 100mg potassium.

ROASTED RED PEPPER HUMMUS

Yield

2 servings

Preparation Time

10 minutes

Cooking Time

0 minutes

INGREDIENTS

- 1/2 can (7.5 oz) chickpeas, drained and rinsed
- 1/4 cup roasted red peppers (jarred or homemade)
- 1 tablespoon tahini
- 1 tablespoon olive oil
- 1/2 clove garlic, minced
- 1/4 teaspoon smoked paprika (optional)
- Salt and pepper to taste
- 1 tablespoon water (optional for thinning)
- Raw veggies for dipping: cucumber slices, carrot sticks, bell pepper slices

DIRECTIONS

1. Blend the hummus. Combine chickpeas, roasted red peppers, tahini, olive oil, garlic, smoked paprika, salt, and pepper in a food processor. Blend until smooth.

2. Adjust texture. If the hummus is too thick, add water 1 teaspoon at a time until it reaches the desired consistency.

3. Transfer to a serving bowl and serve with cucumber slices, carrot sticks, and bell pepper slices.

Nutritional Information: 100 calories, 4g protein, 9g carbohydrates, 5g fat, 2g fiber, 0mg cholesterol, 200mg sodium, 150mg potassium.

QUICK PROTEIN BITES

PEANUT BUTTER OAT ENERGY BALLS

Yield
8 balls

Preparation Time
10 minutes

Cooking Time
0 Minutes

INGREDIENTS

- 1/2 cup old-fashioned oats
- 1/4 cup peanut butter (natural, unsweetened)
- 1 tablespoon honey (or maple syrup)
- 1/2 tablespoon chia seeds (optional)
- 1/4 teaspoon vanilla extract
- Pinch of salt (optional)

DIRECTIONS

1. Mix the ingredients. In a medium bowl, combine the oats, peanut butter, honey, chia seeds (if using), vanilla extract, and a pinch of salt. Stir until everything is well combined.

2. Form the balls. Use your hands to roll the mixture into 8 small balls. If the mixture is too sticky, chill it in the refrigerator for 10-15 minutes before forming the balls.

3. Chill and serve. Place the energy balls in the refrigerator for 30 minutes to firm up. Once chilled, they are ready to enjoy!

Nutritional Information: 110 calories, 4g protein, 12g carbohydrates, 6g fat, 2g fiber, 0mg cholesterol, 40mg sodium, 100mg potassium.

TUNA & AVOCADO SALAD BITES

Yield
2 servings

Preparation Time
10 minutes

Cooking Time
0 Minutes

INGREDIENTS

- 1 can (5 oz) tuna in water, drained
- 1/2 ripe avocado, mashed
- 1 tablespoon lemon juice
- Salt and pepper to taste
- 1 cucumber, sliced into rounds
- Fresh parsley or cilantro for garnish (optional)

DIRECTIONS

1. Make the salad. Combine the drained tuna, mashed avocado, and lemon juice in a small bowl. Mix well, and season with salt and pepper to taste.

2. Assemble the Bites. Place a spoonful of the tuna and avocado mixture onto each cucumber slice.

3. Garnish and serve. If desired, garnish with fresh parsley or cilantro. Serve immediately for a light, refreshing, and protein-packed snack.

Nutritional Information: 180 calories, 20g protein, 8g carbohydrates, 8g fat, 4g fiber, 30mg cholesterol, 250mg sodium, 500mg potassium.

HARD-BOILED EGG & HUMMUS CUPS

Yield
2 servings

Preparation Time
5 minutes

Cooking Time
10 Minutes

INGREDIENTS

- 2 large eggs
- 2 tablespoons hummus
- 1/4 teaspoon paprika (optional)
- Salt and pepper to taste
- Fresh parsley for garnish (optional)

DIRECTIONS

1. Boil the Eggs. Place the eggs in a saucepan and cover with water. Bring to a boil over medium-high heat. Once boiling, remove the eggs from the heat and let them sit in the hot water for 10 minutes. Then, transfer them to a bowl of cold water to cool. Peel the eggs.

2. Assemble the Cups. Cut each egg in half lengthwise. Top each half with a small dollop (about 1/2 tablespoon) of hummus.

3. Sprinkle with paprika and season with salt and pepper. If desired, garnish with fresh parsley and serve.

Nutritional Information: 130 calories, 10g protein, 6g carbohydrates, 8g fat, 1g fiber, 190mg cholesterol, 200mg sodium, 150mg potassium.

ALMOND BUTTER & CHIA SEED BITES

Yield
12 bites

Preparation Time
10 minutes

Cooking Time
20 minutes

INGREDIENTS

- 1/2 cup almond butter
- 1/4 cup chia seeds
- 1/4 cup rolled oats
- 2 tablespoons maple syrup (or sugar-free sweetener)
- 1/2 teaspoon cinnamon
- 1 teaspoon vanilla extract (optional)
- 1 tablespoon water (if needed to adjust consistency)

DIRECTIONS

1. In a mixing bowl, combine almond butter, chia seeds, rolled oats, maple syrup, cinnamon, and vanilla extract (if using). Stir until everything is well combined. Add water if the mixture is too dry.

2. Form the Bites. Roll the mixture into small bite-sized balls, about 1 inch in diameter.

3. Place the bites on a plate or baking sheet and refrigerate for about 20 minutes, or until firm.

4. Enjoy as a quick, on-the-go snack. Leftovers can be stored in an airtight container in the fridge for up to a week.

Nutritional Information: 90 calories, 3g protein, 7g carbohydrates, 6g fat, 3g fiber, 0mg cholesterol, 40mg sodium, 90mg potassium.

GREEK YOGURT & BERRY PROTEIN PARFAITS

Yield

2 servings

Preparation Time

5 minutes

Cooking Time

0 Minutes

INGREDIENTS

- 1 cup plain Greek yogurt (unsweetened)
- 1/2 cup fresh mixed berries (blueberries, strawberries, or raspberries)
- 1 tablespoon chia seeds
- 1 tablespoon honey or maple syrup (optional for sweetness)
- 1/4 cup granola (optional for added crunch)

DIRECTIONS

1. Layer the Ingredients. Add 1/4 cup Greek yogurt to the bottom of two small cups or bowls. Top with a layer of fresh berries and a sprinkle of chia seeds.

2. Add the Second Layer. Repeat the process, adding another 1/4 cup of Greek yogurt to each cup, followed by more berries and chia seeds.

3. Drizzle with honey or maple syrup if desired. Garnish with granola for added crunch (optional). Serve immediately.

Nutritional Information: 160 calories, 12g protein, 22g carbohydrates, 4g fat, 5g fiber, 0mg cholesterol, 60mg sodium, 250mg potassium.

AFFORDABLE LOW-CARB SNACKS

CHEESE & TURKEY ROLL-UPS

Yield
2 servings

Preparation Time
5 minutes

Cooking Time
0 Minutes

INGREDIENTS

- 4 slices deli turkey (thinly sliced)
- 2 slices cheddar or Swiss cheese
- 1 teaspoon mustard (optional)
- Fresh herbs like parsley or chives for garnish (optional)
- Salt and pepper to taste

DIRECTIONS

1. Assemble the Roll-Ups. Lay the turkey slices flat. Place half a slice of cheese on each turkey slice.
2. Add mustard (optional). Spread a thin layer of mustard on the cheese for extra flavor.
3. Gently roll up the turkey slices with the cheese inside. Secure with a toothpick if needed. Garnish with fresh herbs and sprinkle with salt and pepper if desired.
4. Serve immediately for a quick, protein-packed, low-carb snack.

Nutritional Information: 150 calories, 15g protein, 2g carbohydrates, 9g fat, 0g fiber, 45mg cholesterol, 600mg sodium, 100mg potassium.

ROASTED CHICKPEAS

Yield
2 servings

Preparation Time
5 minutes

Cooking Time
30 Minutes

INGREDIENTS

- 1 can (15 oz) chickpeas, drained and rinsed
- 1 tablespoon olive oil
- 1/2 teaspoon paprika
- 1/2 teaspoon garlic powder
- 1/4 teaspoon salt
- 1/4 teaspoon black pepper

DIRECTIONS

1. Preheat your oven to 400°F (200°C).
2. Prepare the chickpeas. Pat the chickpeas dry with a paper towel to remove excess moisture. Spread them evenly on a baking sheet.
3. Drizzle the olive oil over the chickpeas and sprinkle with paprika, garlic powder, salt, and pepper. Toss the coat evenly.
4. Bake in the oven for 25-30 minutes, shaking the pan halfway through, until the chickpeas are golden and crispy.
5. Let the chickpeas cool slightly before serving. Enjoy them warm or at room temperature as a crunchy, low-carb snack.

Nutritional Information: 180 calories, 6g protein, 20g carbohydrates, 7g fat, 6g fiber, 0mg cholesterol, 400mg sodium, 220mg potassium.

CUCUMBER & CREAM CHEESE BITES

Yield
2 servings

Preparation Time
5 minutes

Cooking Time
0 Minutes

INGREDIENTS

- 1 cucumber, sliced into rounds
- 2 tablespoons cream cheese (softened)
- 1 tablespoon fresh chives, chopped
- Salt and pepper to taste

DIRECTIONS

1. Slice the cucumber into rounds about 1/4-inch thick.
2. Add the Cream Cheese. Spread or dollop a small amount (about 1/2 teaspoon) of cream cheese on each cucumber slice.
3. Sprinkle the cream cheese-topped cucumber slices with fresh chives and season with salt and pepper to taste.
4. Serve immediately for a light, refreshing, and creamy low-carb snack.

Nutritional Information: 80 calories, 2g protein, 4g carbohydrates, 6g fat, 0g fiber, 15mg cholesterol, 100mg sodium, 150mg potassium.

ALMONDS & CHEESE PAIRING

Yield
2 servings

Preparation Time
5 minutes

Cooking Time
0 minutes

INGREDIENTS

- 1/4 cup raw almonds
- 2 oz cheddar cheese, sliced
- 1 small apple (optional, for sweetness)
- Fresh rosemary or thyme (optional, for garnish)

DIRECTIONS

1. Divide the almonds into two portions. Slice the cheddar cheese into thin pieces.
2. Arrange the almonds and cheese on a plate. If desired, slice the apple and serve alongside for a balance of sweetness.
3. For an extra flavor boost, add a sprig of fresh rosemary or thyme.

Nutritional Information: 220 calories, 9g protein, 6g carbohydrates, 18g fat, 4g fiber, 25mg cholesterol, 200mg sodium, 120mg potassium.

DEVILED EGGS WITH AVOCADO

Yield
4 servings (8 halves)

Preparation Time
10 minutes

Cooking Time
10 Minutes

INGREDIENTS

- 4 large eggs
- 1/2 ripe avocado
- 1 teaspoon lime juice
- 1/2 teaspoon Dijon mustard
- Salt and pepper to taste
- Paprika for garnish (optional)
- Fresh cilantro or chives for garnish (optional)

DIRECTIONS

1. Place the eggs in a saucepan and cover with water. Bring to a boil over medium-high heat. Once boiling, remove from heat, cover, and let the eggs sit for 10 minutes. Transfer to a bowl of cold water to cool, then peel.
2. Cut the peeled eggs in half lengthwise. Scoop out the yolks and place them in a small bowl. Mash the yolks with the avocado, lime juice, Dijon mustard, salt, and pepper until smooth.
3. Spoon the avocado mixture back into the egg white halves.
4. Sprinkle with paprika and garnish with fresh cilantro or chives if desired. Serve immediately.

Nutritional Information: 130 calories, 7g protein, 4g carbohydrates, 10g fat, 2g fiber, 190mg cholesterol, 150mg sodium, 200mg potassium.

BAKED VEGGIE CHIPS AND FRIES

CRISPY BAKED SWEET POTATO FRIES

Yield
2 servings

Preparation Time
10 minutes

Cooking Time
25 Minutes

INGREDIENTS

- 2 medium sweet potatoes, peeled and cut into thin fries
- 1 tablespoon olive oil
- 1/2 teaspoon paprika
- 1/2 teaspoon garlic powder
- 1/4 teaspoon salt
- 1/4 teaspoon black pepper

DIRECTIONS

1. Preheat your oven to 425°F (220°C). Line a baking sheet with parchment paper.
2. Prepare the Sweet Potatoes. In a large bowl, toss the sweet potato fries with olive oil, paprika, garlic powder, salt, and pepper until evenly coated.
3. Spread the sweet potato fries in a single layer on the prepared baking sheet, making sure they're not touching each other. Bake for 20-25 minutes, flipping halfway through, until the fries are golden and crispy.
4. Remove from the oven and let cool slightly before serving. Enjoy as a healthy, homemade snack or side dish.

Nutritional Information: 180 calories, 2g protein, 30g carbohydrates, 7g fat, 4g fiber, 0mg cholesterol, 250mg sodium, 400mg potassium.

GARLIC PARMESAN ZUCCHINI CHIPS

Yield
2 servings

Preparation Time
10 minutes

Cooking Time
25 Minutes

INGREDIENTS

- 2 medium zucchinis, thinly sliced into rounds
- 1 tablespoon olive oil
- 1/4 cup grated Parmesan cheese
- 1/2 teaspoon garlic powder
- 1/4 teaspoon salt
- 1/4 teaspoon black pepper

DIRECTIONS

1. Preheat your oven to 400°F (200°C). Line a baking sheet with parchment paper.
2. Prepare the Zucchini. In a large bowl, toss the zucchini slices with olive oil, ensuring each slice is evenly coated.
3. Mix the Parmesan cheese, garlic powder, salt, and pepper in a small bowl. Sprinkle the mixture over the zucchini slices, tossing to coat them evenly.
4. Arrange the zucchini slices on the prepared baking sheet in a single layer. Bake for 20-25 minutes or until the chips are golden and crispy. Check halfway through and flip the slices for even cooking.
5. Let the zucchini chips cool slightly before serving. Enjoy them as a light, flavorful snack!

Nutritional Information: 150 calories, 6g protein, 8g carbohydrates, 10g fat, 2g fiber, 10mg cholesterol, 400mg sodium, 450mg potassium.

SPICED CARROT FRIES

Yield
2 servings

Preparation Time
10 minutes

Cooking Time
20 Minutes

INGREDIENTS

- 4 medium carrots, peeled and cut into sticks
- 1 tablespoon olive oil
- 1/2 teaspoon smoked paprika
- 1/4 teaspoon cumin
- 1/4 teaspoon garlic powder
- 1/4 teaspoon salt
- 1/4 teaspoon black pepper

DIRECTIONS

1. Preheat your oven to 425°F (220°C). Line a baking sheet with parchment paper.
2. Place the carrot sticks in a large bowl. Drizzle with olive oil and toss to coat evenly.
3. Mix the smoked paprika, cumin, garlic powder, salt, and black pepper in a small bowl. Sprinkle the spice mixture over the carrots and toss to coat evenly.
4. Spread the seasoned carrot sticks in a single layer on the prepared baking sheet. Bake for 18-20 minutes until the carrots are tender-crisp and slightly browned on the edges, flipping halfway through.
5. Let the carrot fries cool slightly before serving.

Nutritional Information: 120 calories, 2g protein, 15g carbohydrates, 7g fat, 4g fiber, 0mg cholesterol, 350mg sodium, 400mg potassium.

CRISPY KALE CHIPS

Yield
2 servings

Preparation Time
5 minutes

Cooking Time
15 minutes

INGREDIENTS

- 1 bunch of kale, stems removed, and leaves torn into bite-sized pieces
- 1 tablespoon olive oil
- 1/4 teaspoon sea salt (or to taste)

Optional seasonings: 1/4 teaspoon garlic powder, smoked paprika, or nutritional yeast for extra flavor

DIRECTIONS

1. Preheat your oven to 300°F (150°C). Line a baking sheet with parchment paper.
2. Wash and thoroughly dry the kale leaves. Place them in a large bowl.
3. Drizzle the olive oil over the kale and gently massage the leaves with your hands to ensure they are evenly coated. Sprinkle the kale with sea salt and any additional seasonings you prefer, such as garlic powder or smoked paprika. Toss to distribute the seasoning evenly.
4. Spread the kale leaves in a single layer on the prepared baking sheet. Bake for 12-15 minutes, or until the kale is crispy and just beginning to brown on the edges. Keep an eye on them to prevent burning.
5. Let the kale chips cool slightly before serving. Enjoy them immediately as a crunchy, nutrient-packed snack.

Nutritional Information: 70 calories, 2g protein, 7g carbohydrates, 4g fat, 1g fiber, 0mg cholesterol, 100mg sodium, 300mg potassium.

BAKED EGGPLANT CHIPS

Yield
2 servings

Preparation Time
10 minutes

Cooking Time
30 Minutes

INGREDIENTS

- 1 medium eggplant, sliced into thin rounds (about 1/4-inch thick)
- 1 tablespoon olive oil
- 1/2 teaspoon Italian seasoning (a mix of dried oregano, basil, and thyme)
- 1/4 teaspoon garlic powder
- 1/4 teaspoon salt
- 1/4 teaspoon black pepper

DIRECTIONS

1. Preheat your oven to 375°F (190°C). Line a baking sheet with parchment paper.
2. Place the eggplant slices in a large bowl. Drizzle with olive oil and toss to coat evenly.
3. Mix the Italian seasoning, garlic powder, salt, and black pepper in a small bowl. Sprinkle the seasoning mixture over the eggplant slices and toss to coat evenly.
4. Arrange the eggplant slices on the prepared baking sheet in a single layer. Bake for 25-30 minutes, flipping halfway through, until the eggplant is crispy and golden brown. Keep an eye on them towards the end to prevent burning.
5. Let the eggplant chips cool slightly before serving. Enjoy as a savory, low-carb snack or appetizer.

Nutritional Information: 90 calories, 2g protein, 8g carbohydrates, 6g fat, 3g fiber, 0mg cholesterol, 200mg sodium, 350mg potassium.

CHAPTER 7

DESSERT RECIPES

Who says you must spend hours in the kitchen to enjoy a delicious dessert? These quick and easy dessert recipes are here to satisfy your sweet cravings with minimal effort and maximum flavor. Whether you're craving something fruity, creamy, or crunchy, these simple treats can be whipped up in just a few steps using everyday ingredients. They're perfect when you're in the mood for a delightful, guilt-free dessert without the wait!

QUICK AND EASY DESSERT IDEAS

1 FRUIT-BASED SWEET TREATS

Easy and affordable desserts using fresh or frozen fruits, such as baked apples, berry compote, or grilled peaches with a sprinkle of cinnamon.

2 NO-BAKE DESSERTS

Simple, quick, and budget-friendly no-bake options include chia seed pudding, peanut butter energy balls, or yogurt parfaits with a handful of nuts and berries.

3 LOW-SUGAR BAKES

Enjoy affordable, diabetic-friendly baked goods such as almond flour cookies, oat-based fruit bars, and whole wheat banana muffins made using pantry staples.

4 DAIRY DELIGHTS

Easy desserts featuring low-fat yogurt or cottage cheese, such as creamy yogurt with honey and nuts or cottage cheese topped with fruit and cinnamon.

FRUIT-BASED SWEET TREATS

CINNAMON BAKED APPLES

Yield

2 servings

Preparation Time

10 minutes

Cooking Time

25 Minutes

INGREDIENTS

- 2 medium apples (such as Honeycrisp or Granny Smith)
- 1 tablespoon unsweetened apple juice (or water)
- 1 tablespoon chopped walnuts or pecans
- 1/2 teaspoon ground cinnamon
- 1/2 teaspoon vanilla extract
- 1/4 teaspoon ground nutmeg (optional)
- 1 tablespoon raisins or dried cranberries (optional)
- 1 teaspoon melted coconut oil or butter (optional)

DIRECTIONS

1. Preheat your oven to 350°F (175°C). Lightly grease a small baking dish with coconut oil or butter.
2. Core the apples, leaving the bottom intact to hold the filling. You can use a small knife or an apple corer for this. Place the apples in the prepared baking dish.
3. In a small bowl, mix the chopped walnuts or pecans, ground cinnamon, vanilla extract, and nutmeg (if using). If desired, add raisins or dried cranberries for extra sweetness.
4. Stuff the center of each apple with the filling mixture. Drizzle the apples with unsweetened apple juice or water, and if desired, brush the tops with a little melted coconut oil or butter for extra richness.
5. Cover the baking dish with foil and bake the apples for 20 minutes. Then, remove the foil and bake for 5-10 minutes until the apples are tender and the filling is golden.
6. Let the apples cool slightly before serving. Enjoy them warm as a comforting, naturally sweet dessert.

Nutritional Information: 160 calories, 2g protein, 27g carbohydrates, 7g fat, 4g fiber, 0mg cholesterol, 2mg sodium, 230mg potassium.

GRILLED PEACHES WITH CINNAMON

Yield
2 servings

Preparation Time
5 minutes

Cooking Time
8 Minutes

INGREDIENTS

- 2 ripe peaches, halved and pitted
- 1/2 tablespoon olive oil or melted coconut oil
- 1 tablespoon maple syrup or a sugar-free sweetener (optional, for extra sweetness)
- 1/2 teaspoon ground cinnamon
- 1/4 teaspoon vanilla extract (optional)
- A pinch of sea salt (optional)
- Greek yogurt or whipped coconut cream for serving (optional)

DIRECTIONS

1. Preheat your grill to medium-high heat. Brush the cut sides of the peaches with olive oil or melted coconut oil. If desired, drizzle maple syrup or sprinkle a sugar-free sweetener on the peaches for extra caramelization.
2. Place the peach cut side down on the grill. Grill for 4-5 minutes or until you see grill marks and the peaches begin to soften. Flip the peaches and grill for 3 minutes on the other side.
3. Remove the peaches from the grill and place them on a serving platter. While they're still warm, dust each peach half with ground cinnamon. Drizzle with vanilla extract and a pinch of sea salt to enhance the flavors.
4. Serve the grilled peaches warm, either on their own or with a dollop of Greek yogurt or whipped coconut cream for a creamy, delicious contrast.

Nutritional Information: 100 calories, 1g protein, 22g carbohydrates, 3g fat, 3g fiber, 0mg cholesterol, 0mg sodium, 280mg potassium.

BANANA & BERRY DELIGHT

INGREDIENTS

- 1 medium banana, sliced
- 1/2 cup mixed berries (such as strawberries, blueberries, and raspberries)
- 1/2 cup plain Greek yogurt (unsweetened)
- 1 teaspoon honey or maple syrup (optional for extra sweetness)
- 1 tablespoon chopped nuts (such as almonds, walnuts, or pecans)
- 1/2 teaspoon ground cinnamon
- 1/2 teaspoon vanilla extract (optional)
- Fresh mint leaves for garnish (optional)

Yield
2 servings

Preparation Time
5 minutes

Cooking Time
0 Minutes

DIRECTIONS

1. Slice the banana into rounds and set aside. Wash and pat dry the mixed berries.
2. Layer sliced bananas in two small bowls or parfait glasses. Top with a layer of mixed berries.
3. Spoon Greek yogurt over the fruit layers. Drizzle with honey or maple syrup, and sprinkle with ground cinnamon. Add a touch of vanilla extract for extra flavor.
4. Sprinkle the chopped nuts over the top for added crunch. If using, garnish with fresh mint leaves. Serve immediately and enjoy this refreshing, naturally sweet dessert.

Nutritional Information: 160 calories, 5g protein, 28g carbohydrates, 4g fat, 4g fiber, 5mg cholesterol, 35mg sodium, 300mg potassium.

WARM CINNAMON PEARS WITH GREEK YOGURT

Yield
2 servings

Preparation Time
5 minutes

Cooking Time
10 Minutes

INGREDIENTS

- 2 medium pears, sliced
- 1 teaspoon coconut oil or butter
- 1/2 teaspoon ground cinnamon
- 1/4 teaspoon vanilla extract
- 1/2 cup plain Greek yogurt (unsweetened)
- 1 teaspoon honey or maple syrup (optional for extra sweetness)
- A pinch of sea salt (optional)

DIRECTIONS

1. Wash the pears and slice them into thin wedges, removing the core.
2. Heat the coconut oil or butter in a medium skillet over medium heat. Add the pear slices and sauté for 5-7 minutes, or until they soften and caramelize slightly.
3. Sprinkle the ground cinnamon over the pears and add the vanilla extract. Stir gently to coat the pears evenly. Cook for 2-3 minutes until the pears are tender and fragrant.
4. Divide the warm pears between two bowls. Top each serving with a dollop of Greek yogurt. Drizzle with honey or maple syrup if desired, and sprinkle with a pinch of sea salt for added depth of flavor.

Nutritional Information: 150 calories, 5g protein, 28g carbohydrates, 4g fat, 5g fiber, 5mg cholesterol, 20mg sodium, 300mg potassium.

MIXED BERRY COMPOTE

INGREDIENTS

- 2 cups mixed berries (fresh or frozen, such as strawberries, blueberries, raspberries, and blackberries)
- 2 tablespoons fresh lemon juice
- 1 tablespoon water (adjust as needed)
- 1-2 tablespoons maple syrup or a sugar-free sweetener (such as stevia or other you use)
- 1/2 teaspoon vanilla extract
- 1/2 teaspoon ground cinnamon (optional)
- Zest of 1 lemon (optional, for extra flavor)

Yield
2 servings

Preparation Time
5 minutes

Cooking Time
15 Minutes

DIRECTIONS

1. Prepare the Berries. If using fresh berries, rinse them thoroughly and remove any stems or leaves. If using frozen berries, you can add them directly to the saucepan without thawing.
2. Combine the mixed berries, lemon juice, water, and maple syrup or sweetener in a medium saucepan. Cook over medium heat, stirring occasionally, until the berries begin to break down and release their juices, about 10 minutes. If the mixture is too thick, add additional water, 1 tablespoon at a time, until the desired consistency is reached.
3. Stir in the vanilla extract; if desired, add ground cinnamon and lemon zest for extra depth of flavor. Cook for another 5 minutes or until the compote has thickened slightly.
4. Remove the saucepan from the heat and let the compote cool slightly. Serve warm or at room temperature over yogurt or pancakes or enjoy on its own as a delicious and versatile dessert topping.

Nutritional Information: 60 calories, 1g protein, 14g carbohydrates, 0g fat, 4g fiber, 0mg cholesterol, 2mg sodium, 120mg potassium.

NO-BAKE DESSERTS

VANILLA CHIA SEED PUDDING

Yield
2 servings

Preparation Time
5 minutes

Chill Time
4 hours (or overnight)

INGREDIENTS

- 1/4 cup chia seeds
- 1 cup unsweetened almond milk (or your preferred milk)
- 1/2 teaspoon vanilla extract
- 1-2 teaspoons maple syrup or a sugar-free sweetener (optional, to taste)
- Fresh berries, nuts, or shredded coconut for topping (optional)

DIRECTIONS

1. In a medium-sized bowl or jar, combine the chia seeds, almond milk, vanilla extract, and maple syrup or sweetener (if using). Stir well to ensure the chia seeds are evenly distributed and not clamped together.
2. Cover the bowl or jar and refrigerate for at least 4 hours or overnight. During this time, the chia seeds absorb the liquid and thicken into a pudding-like consistency. Stir the mixture once or twice during the first hour to prevent clumping.
3. Once the pudding has been set, give it a good stir. Divide the pudding into two serving bowls or jars. If desired, top with fresh berries, nuts, or shredded coconut, and enjoy!

Nutritional Information: 150 calories, 5g protein, 15g carbohydrates, 8g fat, 10g fiber, 0mg cholesterol, 120mg sodium, 180mg potassium.

COCONUT CHOCOLATE BITES

Yield
10 bites

Preparation Time
10 minutes

Chill Time
30 minutes

INGREDIENTS

- 1 cup unsweetened shredded coconut
- 2 tablespoons cocoa powder
- 2 tablespoons maple syrup (or a sugar-free sweetener)
- 2 tablespoons coconut oil, melted
- 1/2 teaspoon vanilla extract
- A pinch of sea salt (optional)
- Additional shredded coconut for rolling (optional)

DIRECTIONS

1. Combine the shredded coconut, cocoa powder, maple syrup, melted coconut oil, vanilla extract, and a pinch of sea salt in a medium bowl. Stir until all ingredients are well combined and the mixture holds together when pressed.
2. Scoop out about 1 tablespoon of the mixture and roll it into a ball using your hands. If desired, roll the ball in additional shredded coconut to coat. Repeat with the remaining mixture.
3. Place the coconut chocolate bites on a plate or tray lined with parchment paper. Refrigerate for at least 30 minutes to allow them to firm up.
4. Once chilled, the bites are ready to enjoy. Store any leftovers in an airtight container in the refrigerator for up to a week.

Nutritional Information: 90 calories, 1g protein, 6g carbohydrates, 7g fat, 3g fiber, 0mg cholesterol, 5mg sodium, 60mg potassium.

LEMON COCONUT BLISS BALLS

Yield
10 balls

Preparation Time
10 minutes

Chill Time
30 Minutes

INGREDIENTS

- 1 cup unsweetened shredded coconut
- 2 tablespoons coconut flour (or almond flour)
- 2 tablespoons coconut oil, melted
- 2 tablespoons maple syrup (or a sugar-free sweetener)
- Zest of 1 lemon
- 1 tablespoon fresh lemon juice
- 1/2 teaspoon vanilla extract
- A pinch of sea salt (optional)
- Additional shredded coconut for rolling (optional)

DIRECTIONS

1. In a medium bowl, combine the shredded coconut, coconut flour, melted coconut oil, maple syrup, lemon zest, lemon juice, vanilla extract, and a pinch of sea salt if using. Stir until the mixture is well combined and holds together when pressed.

2. Scoop out about 1 tablespoon of the mixture and roll it into a ball using your hands. If desired, roll the ball in additional shredded coconut to coat. Repeat with the remaining mixture.

3. Place the lemon coconut bliss balls on a plate or tray lined with parchment paper. Refrigerate for at least 30 minutes to allow them to firm up.

4. Once chilled, the bliss balls are ready to enjoy. Store any leftovers in an airtight container in the refrigerator for up to a week.

Nutritional Information: 80 calories, 1g protein, 6g carbohydrates, 6g fat, 2g fiber, 0mg cholesterol, 5mg sodium, 40mg potassium.

ALMOND BUTTER BANANA BITES

Yield
2 servings

Preparation Time
5 minutes

Chill Time
15 minutes

INGREDIENTS

- 1 medium banana, sliced into rounds
- 2 tablespoons almond butter
- 1 teaspoon chia seeds
- A drizzle of honey or maple syrup (optional)
- A pinch of sea salt (optional)

DIRECTIONS

1. Slice the banana into rounds about 1/2 inch thick and arrange them on a plate or tray.

2. Top each banana slice with a slight almond butter dollop (about 1/4 teaspoon).

3. Lightly sprinkle chia seeds over the almond butter-topped banana slices. If desired, drizzle with honey or maple syrup for added sweetness and add a pinch of sea salt for extra flavor.

4. Place the plate or tray in the refrigerator for about 15 minutes to allow the almond butter to firm up and the flavors to meld.

5. Enjoy the banana bites as a quick, refreshing, and nutritious no-bake dessert.

Nutritional Information: 150 calories, 3g protein, 20g carbohydrates, 7g fat, 4g fiber, 0mg cholesterol, 25mg sodium, 300mg potassium.

MINT CHOCOLATE AVOCADO MOUSSE

Yield
2 servings

Preparation Time
10 minutes

Chill Time
30 Minutes

INGREDIENTS

- 1 ripe avocado
- 2 tablespoons unsweetened cocoa powder
- 2 tablespoons maple syrup or a sugar-free sweetener
- 1/4 teaspoon peppermint extract (or 4-5 fresh mint leaves, finely chopped)
- 1/4 teaspoon vanilla extract
- A pinch of sea salt
- Fresh mint leaves or dark chocolate shavings for garnish (optional)

DIRECTIONS

1. Cut the avocado in half, remove the pit, and scoop the flesh into a blender or food processor.

2. Add the unsweetened cocoa powder, maple syrup or sweetener, peppermint extract (or chopped fresh mint leaves), vanilla extract, and a pinch of sea salt to the blender. Blend until the mixture is smooth and creamy, stopping to scrape down the sides as needed.

3. Taste the mousse and adjust the sweetness or mint flavor by adding more maple syrup or peppermint extract.

4. Divide the mousse into two small bowls or ramekins. Cover and refrigerate for at least 30 minutes to allow the flavors to meld and the mousse to firm up slightly.

5. Garnish with fresh mint leaves or dark chocolate shavings if desired. Serve chilled, and enjoy this rich, creamy, and refreshing dessert.

Nutritional Information: 180 calories, 3g protein, 15g carbohydrates, 14g fat, 7g fiber, 0mg cholesterol, 60mg sodium, 500mg potassium.

LOW-SUGAR BAKES

CINNAMON APPLE OAT COOKIES

Yield
12 cookies

Preparation Time
10 minutes

Cooking Time
15 minutes

INGREDIENTS

- 1 cup rolled oats
- 1/2 cup whole wheat flour
- 1 teaspoon baking powder
- 1 teaspoon ground cinnamon
- 1/4 teaspoon ground nutmeg (optional)
- 1/4 teaspoon sea salt
- 1/4 cup coconut oil or unsalted butter, melted
- 1/4 cup maple syrup or sugar-free sweetener (adjust to taste)
- 1 large egg, beaten
- 1 teaspoon vanilla extract
- 1 medium apple, peeled, cored, and diced
- 1/4 cup chopped walnuts or pecans (optional)

DIRECTIONS

1. Preheat your oven to 350°F (175°C). Line a baking sheet with parchment paper or lightly grease it.
2. In a large bowl, combine the rolled oats, whole wheat flour, baking powder, ground cinnamon, ground nutmeg (if using), and sea salt.
3. In a separate bowl, whisk together the melted coconut oil or butter, maple syrup or sugar-free sweetener, beaten egg, and vanilla extract until well combined.
4. Form the Dough. Pour the wet ingredients into the dry ingredients and stir until just combined. Gently fold in the diced apple and chopped nuts if using.
5. Shape the Cookies. Scoop out about 1 tablespoon of dough per cookie and place them on the prepared baking sheet, flattening them slightly with your hand or the back of a spoon.
6. Bake the cookies for 12-15 minutes or until the edges are golden and the cookies are set. Remove from the oven and allow them to cool on the baking sheet for a few minutes before transferring to a wire rack to cool completely.

Nutritional Information: 115 calories, 2g protein, 18g carbohydrates, 5g fat, 2g fiber, 15mg cholesterol, 70mg sodium, 80mg potassium.

WHOLE WHEAT BANANA NUT MUFFINS

Yield
12 muffins

Preparation Time
10 minutes

Cooking Time
20 Minutes

INGREDIENTS

- 1 1/2 cups whole wheat flour
- 1 teaspoon baking soda
- 1/2 teaspoon ground cinnamon
- 1/4 teaspoon sea salt
- 3 ripe bananas, mashed
- 1/3 cup maple syrup (or a sugar-free sweetener)
- 1/4 cup melted coconut oil or vegetable oil
- 1 large egg, beaten
- 1 teaspoon vanilla extract
- 1/2 cup chopped walnuts or pecans

DIRECTIONS

1. Preheat your oven to 350°F (175°C). Line a 12-cup muffin tin with paper liners or lightly grease the cups.
2. Whisk together the whole wheat flour, baking soda, ground cinnamon, and sea salt in a large bowl.
3. In a separate bowl, mix the mashed bananas, maple syrup or a sugar-free sweetener, melted coconut oil, beaten egg, and vanilla extract until smooth.
4. Form the Batter. Pour the wet ingredients into the dry ingredients and stir until just combined. Fold in the chopped nuts, being careful not to overmix.
5. Bake the Muffins. Divide the batter evenly among the muffin cups, filling each about 3/4 full. Bake for 18-20 minutes, or until a toothpick inserted into the center of a muffin comes out clean.
6. Allow the muffins to cool in the tin briefly before transferring to a wire rack to cool completely. Enjoy warm or at room temperature.

Nutritional Information: 180 calories, 4g protein, 27g carbohydrates, 7g fat, 3g fiber, 20mg cholesterol, 100mg sodium, 200mg potassium.

OAT & BLUEBERRY BREAKFAST BARS

INGREDIENTS

- 2 cups rolled oats
- 1/2 teaspoon baking powder
- 1/2 teaspoon ground cinnamon
- 1/4 teaspoon sea salt
- 1/2 cup unsweetened applesauce
- 1/4 cup honey (or a sugar-free sweetener)
- 1 large egg, beaten
- 1 teaspoon vanilla extract
- 1/2 cup fresh or frozen blueberries
- 1/4 cup chopped nuts (optional, for added crunch)

Yield
9 bars

Preparation Time
10 minutes

Cooking Time
25 Minutes

DIRECTIONS

1. Preheat your oven to 350°F (175°C). Line a baking dish with parchment paper or lightly grease it.
2. In a large bowl, combine the rolled oats, baking powder, ground cinnamon, and sea salt. In a separate bowl, mix the applesauce, honey, beaten egg, and vanilla extract until well combined.
3. Pour the wet ingredients into the dry ingredients and stir until combined. Gently fold in the blueberries and chopped nuts if using.
4. Spread the batter evenly in the prepared baking dish. Bake for 20-25 minutes until the edges are golden brown and a toothpick inserted into the center comes clean.
5. Allow the bars to cool in the pan before cutting into squares. Store any leftovers in an airtight container in the refrigerator for up to a week.

Nutritional Information: 150 calories, 3g protein, 24g carbohydrates, 5g fat, 3g fiber, 20mg cholesterol, 80mg sodium, 110mg potassium.

PUMPKIN SPICE ALMOND LOAF

Yield
1 loaf (8 slices)

Preparation Time
10 minutes

Cooking Time
45 Minutes

INGREDIENTS

- 2 cups almond flour
- 1/2 teaspoon baking soda
- 1/2 teaspoon baking powder
- 1 tablespoon pumpkin pie spice
- 1/4 teaspoon ground cinnamon
- 1/4 teaspoon sea salt
- 3/4 cup pumpkin puree (unsweetened)
- 1/4 cup maple syrup or a sugar-free sweetener
- 2 large eggs
- 1/4 cup coconut oil, melted
- 1 teaspoon vanilla extract
- 1/4 cup chopped nuts or seeds (optional)

DIRECTIONS

1. Preheat your oven to 350°F (175°C). Grease a loaf pan or line it with parchment paper.

2. In a large bowl, whisk the almond flour, baking soda, baking powder, pumpkin pie spice, ground cinnamon, and sea salt until well combined.

3. In a separate bowl, whisk together the pumpkin puree, maple syrup or sugar-free sweetener, eggs, melted coconut oil, and vanilla extract until smooth and well combined.

4. Form the Batter. Pour the wet ingredients into the dry ingredients and stir until just combined. If using, fold in the chopped nuts or seeds.

5. Pour the batter into the prepared loaf pan, smoothing the top with a spatula. Bake for 40-45 minutes or until a toothpick inserted into the center comes clean.

6. Allow the loaf to cool in the pan for 10 minutes, then transfer it to a wire rack to cool completely. Slice and serve. Store any leftovers in an airtight container at room temperature for 3 days.

Nutritional Information: 200 calories, 6g protein, 12g carbohydrates, 16g fat, 4g fiber, 40mg cholesterol, 180mg sodium, 160mg potassium.

ALMOND FLOUR CHOCOLATE CHIP COOKIES

Yield
12 cookies

Preparation Time
10 minutes

Cooking Time
12 Minutes

INGREDIENTS

- 2 cups almond flour
- 1/4 teaspoon baking soda
- 1/4 teaspoon sea salt
- 1/4 cup coconut oil, melted
- 1/4 cup maple syrup (or a sugar-free sweetener)
- 1 teaspoon vanilla extract
- 1/3 cup sugar-free chocolate chips (or dark chocolate chips)

DIRECTIONS

1. Preheat your oven to 350°F (175°C). Line a baking sheet with parchment paper.
2. Whisk the almond flour, baking soda, and sea salt in a large bowl until well combined.
3. Mix the melted coconut oil, maple syrup, and vanilla extract in a separate bowl until smooth.
4. Pour the wet ingredients into the dry ingredients and stir until dough forms. Fold in the chocolate chips.
5. Scoop about 1 tablespoon of dough per cookie and roll into balls. Place the balls onto the prepared baking sheet and gently flatten them with your hand or the back of a spoon to form cookie shapes.
6. Bake the cookies for 10-12 minutes, or until the edges are golden brown. Remove them from the oven and let them cool on the baking sheet for a few minutes before transferring them to a wire rack to cool completely.

Nutritional Information: 130 calories, 3g protein, 9g carbohydrates, 10g fat, 2g fiber, 0mg cholesterol, 60mg sodium, 90mg potassium.

DAIRY DELIGHTS

MAPLE-NUT GREEK YOGURT

Yield
2 servings

Preparation Time
5 minutes

Cooking Time
0 Minutes

INGREDIENTS

- 1 cup plain Greek yogurt (unsweetened)
- 2 tablespoons maple syrup (or a sugar-free sweetener)
- 1/4 cup mixed nuts (such as almonds, walnuts, and pecans), chopped
- 1/2 teaspoon vanilla extract (optional)
- A pinch of ground cinnamon (optional)

DIRECTIONS

1. In a medium bowl, stir the Greek yogurt until smooth and creamy. If using, mix in the vanilla extract for added flavor.
2. Drizzle 1 tablespoon of maple syrup over each serving of yogurt.
3. Sprinkle the chopped mixed nuts evenly over the top of the yogurt.
4. Add a pinch of ground cinnamon for extra warmth and flavor if desired. Serve immediately and enjoy this simple, protein-rich dessert.

Nutritional Information: 200 calories, 10g protein, 18g carbohydrates, 10g fat, 2g fiber, 0mg cholesterol, 50mg sodium, 250mg potassium.

YOGURT & ALMOND BUTTER SWIRL

Yield
2 servings

Preparation Time
5 minutes

Cooking Time
0 minutes

INGREDIENTS

- 1 cup plain low-fat yogurt (Greek or regular)
- 2 tablespoons almond butter
- 1 teaspoon maple syrup or a sugar-free sweetener (optional)
- 1 teaspoon chia seeds
- A pinch of ground cinnamon (optional)

DIRECTIONS

1. Divide the yogurt evenly between two small bowls.
2. Drizzle 1 tablespoon of almond butter over each serving of yogurt. If needed, soften the almond butter slightly in the microwave for 10-15 seconds, making it easier to swirl.
3. Using a spoon, gently swirl the almond butter into the yogurt to create a marbled effect.
4. Sprinkle the chia seeds evenly over each serving. If desired, add a pinch of ground cinnamon for extra flavor.
5. Enjoy immediately as a quick, protein-packed dessert or snack.

Nutritional Information: 190 calories, 10g protein, 12g carbohydrates, 13g fat, 3g fiber, 0mg cholesterol, 50mg sodium, 300mg potassium.

SPICED APPLE COTTAGE CHEESE BOWL

Yield
2 servings

Preparation Time
5 minutes

Cooking Time
10 Minutes

INGREDIENTS

- 1 large apple, peeled, cored, and diced
- 1/2 teaspoon ground cinnamon
- 1/4 teaspoon ground nutmeg (optional)
- 1 teaspoon coconut oil or butter
- 1 teaspoon maple syrup or a sugar-free sweetener (optional)
- 1 cup low-fat cottage cheese
- 1 tablespoon chopped walnuts or pecans (optional, for topping)

DIRECTIONS

1. Heat the coconut oil or butter over medium heat in a small skillet. Add the diced apple, ground cinnamon, and ground nutmeg. Cook for 5-7 minutes, stirring occasionally, until the apples are tender and fragrant. If desired, drizzle with maple syrup or a sugar-free sweetener and stir to coat.
2. While the apples are cooking, divide the cottage cheese between two bowls.
3. Once the apples are done, spoon them over the cottage cheese in each bowl.
4. If desired, sprinkle chopped walnuts or pecans on top for added crunch. Serve warm and enjoy this comforting, balanced treat.

Nutritional Information: 180 calories, 10g protein, 20g carbohydrates, 7g fat, 3g fiber, 10mg cholesterol, 350mg sodium, 250mg potassium.

TROPICAL COCONUT YOGURT BOWL

Yield
2 servings

Preparation Time
5 minutes

Cooking Time
0 Minutes

INGREDIENTS

- 1 cup plain low-fat yogurt (Greek or regular)
- 1/2 cup diced pineapple (fresh or canned in juice, drained; ensure canned pineapple has no added sugar)
- 2 tablespoons unsweetened shredded coconut
- 1 teaspoon honey or maple syrup (optional)
- A few fresh mint leaves for garnish (optional)

DIRECTIONS

1. Divide the yogurt evenly between two bowls.
2. Top each serving of yogurt with 1/4 cup diced pineapple and 1 tablespoon shredded coconut.
3. If desired, drizzle 1/2 teaspoon of honey or maple syrup over each bowl for a touch of sweetness.
4. Garnish with fresh mint leaves if desired. Serve immediately and enjoy this tropical, refreshing dessert.

Nutritional Information: 170 calories, 8g protein, 24g carbohydrates, 6g fat, 2g fiber, 5mg cholesterol, 50mg sodium, 250mg potassium.

COTTAGE CHEESE & BERRY PARFAIT

Yield

2 servings

Preparation Time

5 minutes

Cooking Time

0 minutes

INGREDIENTS

- 1 cup low-fat cottage cheese
- 1 cup mixed berries (such as strawberries, blueberries, and raspberries)
- 2 teaspoons maple syrup or a sugar-free sweetener (optional)
- 1/4 cup granola or chopped nuts (optional, for added crunch)
- Fresh mint leaves for garnish (optional)

DIRECTIONS

1. Wash and pat dry the mixed berries. If desired, slice any larger berries like strawberries.
2. Add a layer of cottage cheese (about 1/4 cup each) in two serving glasses or bowls. Top with a layer of mixed berries (about 1/4 cup each).
3. Add sweetener (optional): If desired, drizzle 1 teaspoon of maple syrup or a sugar-free sweetener over each serving.
4. Repeat layers. Add another layer of cottage cheese and berries to each glass or bowl. If using, sprinkle granola or chopped nuts on top for added crunch.
5. Garnish with fresh mint leaves if desired. Serve immediately and enjoy this light and refreshing parfait.

Nutritional Information: 150 calories, 10g protein, 20g carbohydrates, 4g fat, 3g fiber, 10mg cholesterol, 350mg sodium, 250mg potassium.

CHAPTER 8

BEVERAGE RECIPES

S taying hydrated is super essential for keeping our bodies healthy, and what better way to do it than by treating ourselves to a variety of yummy, refreshing drinks? In this excellent section, you'll find a bunch of drink recipes that are not only delicious but also perfect for those following a diabetic-friendly lifestyle. From energizing smoothies and calming teas to rejuvenating infused waters, these drinks are a breeze and crafted with simple, wholesome ingredients. Whether you need a morning boost, a relaxing evening beverage, or just a pick-me-up during the day, these drinks are simply perfect for any occasion!

QUICK AND EASY BEVERAGE IDEAS

1 LOW-SUGAR SMOOTHIES

Easy-to-make smoothies using affordable ingredients like frozen berries, spinach, bananas, and plain yogurt, with optional add-ins like chia seeds or almond milk.

2 INFUSED WATER AND ICED TEAS

Refreshing and budget-friendly beverages like cucumber-lemon water, mint, and berry-infused water, or unsweetened iced green tea with a squeeze of lemon.

3 HEALTHY WARM DRINKS

Simple, comforting beverages such as cinnamon-spiced almond milk, turmeric tea, or sugar-free hot chocolate made with cocoa powder and low-fat dairy.

4 FRUIT AND VEGGIE JUICES

Affordable homemade juices made with ingredients like carrots, apples, and spinach blended for a nutrient-packed drink without added sugar.

LOW-SUGAR SMOOTHIES

BERRY BANANA BLISS SMOOTHIE

INGREDIENTS

- 1 cup frozen mixed berries (such as strawberries, blueberries, and raspberries)
- 1 ripe banana
- 1/2 cup plain yogurt (Greek or regular)
- 1/2 cup unsweetened almond milk (or any milk of your choice)
- 1/2 teaspoon vanilla extract (optional)
- Ice cubes (optional, for a thicker smoothie)

Yield
2 servings

Preparation Time
5 minutes

Cooking Time
0 Minutes

DIRECTIONS

1. Peel and slice the ripe banana.
2. Combine the frozen mixed berries, sliced banana, plain yogurt, and almond milk in a blender. Add vanilla extract if using. Blend on high until smooth and creamy. If you prefer a thicker smoothie, add a few ice cubes and blend until smooth.
3. Pour the smoothie into two glasses and serve immediately. Enjoy this naturally sweet and refreshing smoothie as a quick breakfast or snack.

Nutritional Information: 150 calories, 4g protein, 30g carbohydrates, 2g fat, 5g fiber, 0mg cholesterol, 55mg sodium, 400mg potassium.

GREEN POWER SPINACH SMOOTHIE

INGREDIENTS

- 1 cup fresh spinach, packed
- 1 ripe banana
- 1/2 cup unsweetened almond milk (or any milk of your choice)
- 1/2 cup plain Greek yogurt (optional for added protein and creaminess)
- 1/2 teaspoon vanilla extract (optional)
- 1 tablespoon chia seeds (optional, for extra fiber and omega-3s)
- Ice cubes (optional for a thicker smoothie)

Yield
2 servings

Preparation Time
5 minutes

Cooking Time
0 Minutes

DIRECTIONS

1. Peel and slice the ripe banana.
2. In a blender, combine the fresh spinach, sliced banana, almond milk, and Greek yogurt if using. Add vanilla extract and chia seeds if desired. Blend on high until smooth and creamy. If you prefer a thicker smoothie, add a few ice cubes and blend until smooth.
3. Pour the smoothie into two glasses and serve immediately. Enjoy this vibrant and nutritious smoothie as a refreshing and energizing start to your day.

Nutritional Information: 140 calories, 6g protein, 26g carbohydrates, 3g fat, 4g fiber, 5mg cholesterol, 60mg sodium, 450mg potassium.

PEANUT BUTTER BANANA PROTEIN SMOOTHIE

INGREDIENTS

- 1 ripe banana
- 2 tablespoons natural peanut butter
- 1/2 cup unsweetened almond milk (or any milk of your choice)
- 1/2 cup plain Greek yogurt (for added protein and creaminess)
- 1 scoop vanilla protein powder (optional, for extra protein)
- 1/2 teaspoon vanilla extract (optional)
- Ice cubes (optional, for a thicker smoothie)

Yield
2 servings

Preparation Time
5 minutes

Cooking Time
0 Minutes

DIRECTIONS

1. Peel and slice the ripe banana.
2. Blend the Smoothie. In a blender, combine the sliced banana, peanut butter, almond milk, Greek yogurt, and protein powder if using. Add vanilla extract if desired. Blend on high until smooth and creamy. If you prefer a thicker smoothie, add a few ice cubes and blend until smooth.
3. Pour the smoothie into two glasses and serve immediately. Enjoy this creamy, protein-packed smoothie as a post-workout recovery drink or a satisfying snack.

Nutritional Information: 250 calories, 15g protein, 30g carbohydrates, 10g fat, 4g fiber, 10mg cholesterol, 120mg sodium, 500mg potassium.

TROPICAL MANGO COCONUT SMOOTHIE

Yield
2 servings

Preparation Time
5 minutes

Cooking Time
0 minutes

INGREDIENTS

- 1 cup frozen mango chunks
- 1/2 cup unsweetened coconut milk (from a carton, not canned)
- 1/2 cup plain Greek yogurt (optional, for added creaminess and protein)
- 1/2 teaspoon vanilla extract (optional)
- 1 tablespoon unsweetened shredded coconut (optional, for garnish)
- Ice cubes (optional, for a thicker smoothie)

DIRECTIONS

1. Measure out the frozen mango chunks.
2. In a blender, combine the frozen mango chunks, coconut milk, and Greek yogurt if using. Add vanilla extract if desired. Blend on high until smooth and creamy. If you prefer a thicker smoothie, add a few ice cubes and blend until smooth.
3. Pour the smoothie into two glasses. If desired, garnish with a sprinkle of shredded coconut on top. Serve immediately and enjoy this creamy, tropical drink.

Nutritional Information: 160 calories, 4g protein, 25g carbohydrates, 6g fat, 3g fiber, 0mg cholesterol, 50mg sodium, 300mg potassium.

CHIA BERRY YOGURT SMOOTHIE

Yield
2 servings

Preparation Time
5 minutes

Cooking Time
0 Minutes

INGREDIENTS

- 1 cup frozen mixed berries (such as strawberries, blueberries, and raspberries)
- 1/2 cup plain Greek yogurt
- 1/2 cup unsweetened almond milk (or any milk of your choice)
- 1 tablespoon chia seeds
- 1/2 teaspoon vanilla extract (optional)
- 1-2 teaspoons maple syrup or a sugar-free sweetener (optional, for added sweetness)
- Ice cubes (optional, for a thicker smoothie)

DIRECTIONS

1. Measure out the frozen berries and chia seeds.
2. In a blender, combine the frozen mixed berries, Greek yogurt, almond milk, chia seeds, and vanilla extract if using. Add maple syrup or sweetener if desired. Blend on high until smooth and creamy. If you prefer a thicker smoothie, add a few ice cubes and blend again until smooth.
3. Pour the smoothie into two glasses and serve immediately. Enjoy this thick, filling, and nutritious smoothie as a satisfying snack or meal replacement.

Nutritional Information: 180 calories, 8g protein, 24g carbohydrates, 7g fat, 8g fiber, 5mg cholesterol, 70mg sodium, 350mg potassium.

INFUSED WATER AND ICED TEAS

CUCUMBER LEMON REFRESHMENT

Yield
2 servings

Preparation Time
5 minutes

Infusion Time
1-2 hours

INGREDIENTS

- 4 cups cold water
- 1/2 cucumber, thinly sliced
- 1/2 lemon, thinly sliced
- A few fresh mint leaves (optional for added freshness)
- Ice cubes (optional for serving)

DIRECTIONS

1. Thinly slice the cucumber and lemon. If using, gently crush the mint leaves to release their flavor.
2. In a large pitcher, combine the cold water with the cucumber slices, lemon slices, and mint leaves if using. Stir to combine.
3. Cover the pitcher and refrigerate for 1-2 hours to allow the flavors to infuse into the water. For a more robust flavor, you can let it infuse overnight.
4. When ready to serve, pour the infused water into glasses over ice cubes if desired. Enjoy this crisp and hydrating drink, perfect for cooling off on a hot day.

Nutritional Information: 5 calories, 0g protein, 1g carbohydrates, 0g fat, 0g fiber, 0mg cholesterol, 2mg sodium, 15mg potassium.

MINTY CUCUMBER LIME WATER

Yield
2 servings

Preparation Time
5 minutes

Infusion Time
1-2 hours

INGREDIENTS

- 4 cups cold water
- 1/2 cucumber, thinly sliced
- 1/2 lime, thinly sliced
- A handful of fresh mint leaves
- Ice cubes (optional for serving)

DIRECTIONS

1. Thinly slice the cucumber and lime. Gently crush the mint leaves to release their natural oils.
2. In a large pitcher, combine the cold water with the cucumber slices, lime slices, and mint leaves. Stir gently to mix the flavors.
3. Cover the pitcher and refrigerate for 1-2 hours to allow the flavors to infuse into the water. For a stronger flavor, you can let it infuse overnight.
4. When ready to serve, pour the infused water into glasses over ice cubes if desired. Enjoy this cooling and hydrating drink throughout the day.

Nutritional Information: 5 calories, 0g protein, 1g carbohydrates, 0g fat, 0g fiber, 0mg cholesterol, 2mg sodium, 15mg potassium.

MINT AND BERRY INFUSION

Yield
2 servings

Preparation Time
5 minutes

Infusion Time
1-2 hours

INGREDIENTS

- 4 cups cold water
- 1/2 cup mixed berries (such as strawberries, blueberries, and raspberries)
- A handful of fresh mint leaves
- Ice cubes (optional for serving)

DIRECTIONS

1. Gently rinse the mixed berries and mint leaves. Slightly crush the mint leaves to release their natural oils.
2. Infuse the Water. Combine the cold water with the mixed berries and mint leaves in a large pitcher. Stir gently to mix.
3. Cover the pitcher and refrigerate for 1-2 hours to allow the flavors to infuse into the water. For a more robust flavor, you can let it infuse overnight.
4. When ready to serve, pour the infused water into glasses over ice cubes if desired. Enjoy this naturally sweet and flavorful drink, perfect for staying hydrated throughout the day.

Nutritional Information: 10 calories, 0g protein, 2g carbohydrates, 0g fat, 1g fiber, 0mg cholesterol, 1mg sodium, 25mg potassium.

CITRUS GREEN ICED TEA

Yield
2 servings

Preparation Time
5 minutes

Brew Time
5 minutes

Chill Time
30 minutes

INGREDIENTS

- 2 cups water
- 2 green tea bags (or 2 teaspoons loose-leaf green tea)
- 1/2 lemon, thinly sliced
- 1/2 orange, thinly sliced
- 1 tablespoon fresh lemon juice
- Ice cubes (for serving)
- Fresh mint leaves (optional, for garnish)

DIRECTIONS

1. In a small saucepan, bring the water to a boil. Remove from heat and add the green tea bags. Let the tea steep for 3-5 minutes, depending on your preferred strength.
2. Remove the tea bags and allow the tea to cool slightly. Then, pour the brewed tea into a large pitcher and refrigerate for about 30 minutes, or until well chilled.
3. Once the tea is chilled, add the lemon slices, orange slices, and fresh lemon juice. Stir to combine.
4. Fill two glasses with ice cubes, then pour the citrus green iced tea over the ice. Garnish with fresh mint leaves if desired. Serve immediately and enjoy this refreshing, antioxidant-rich drink.

Nutritional Information: 10 calories, 0g protein, 3g carbohydrates, 0g fat, 0g fiber, 0mg cholesterol, 0mg sodium, 50mg potassium.

BERRY HIBISCUS ICED TEA

Yield
2 servings

Preparation Time
5 minutes

Brew Time
10 minutes

Chill Time
30 minutes

INGREDIENTS

- 2 cups water
- 2 hibiscus tea bags (or 2 tablespoons dried hibiscus flowers)
- 1/2 cup fresh mixed berries (such as strawberries, blueberries, and raspberries)
- 1 tablespoon fresh lemon juice (optional, for added tanginess)
- Ice cubes (for serving)
- Fresh mint leaves or additional berries (optional, for garnish)

DIRECTIONS

1. Brew the Hibiscus Tea. In a small saucepan, bring the water to a boil. Remove from heat and add the hibiscus tea bags or dried hibiscus flowers. Let it steep for 10 minutes, allowing the tea to develop a deep, vibrant color and tangy flavor.

2. If using dried hibiscus flowers, strain the tea to remove the flowers. Allow the tea to cool slightly, pour it into a large pitcher, and refrigerate for about 30 minutes or until well chilled.

3. Once the tea is chilled, add the fresh mixed berries and lemon juice if using. Stir gently to combine, allowing the berries to infuse flavor into the tea.

4. Fill two glasses with ice cubes, then pour the berry hibiscus iced tea over the ice. Garnish with fresh mint leaves or additional berries if desired. Serve immediately and enjoy this vibrant, tangy, and naturally caffeine-free drink.

Nutritional Information: 20 calories, 0g protein, 5g carbohydrates, 0g fat, 1g fiber, 0mg cholesterol, 0mg sodium, 50mg potassium.

HEALTHY WARM DRINKS

CINNAMON-SPICED ALMOND MILK

Yield
2 servings

Preparation Time
2 minutes

Cooking Time
5 Minutes

INGREDIENTS

- 2 cups unsweetened almond milk
- 1/2 teaspoon ground cinnamon
- 1/2 teaspoon vanilla extract
- 1-2 teaspoons maple syrup or a sugar-free sweetener (optional for added sweetness)
- A pinch of ground nutmeg (optional for extra warmth)

DIRECTIONS

1. Place the almond milk into a small saucepan over medium heat. Warm the milk, stirring occasionally, until it's hot but not boiling (about 3-5 minutes).
2. Stir in the ground cinnamon, vanilla extract, and maple syrup or sweetener if using. If desired, add a pinch of ground nutmeg for extra warmth.
3. Pour the warm, spiced almond milk into two mugs. Stir well to ensure the spices are evenly distributed. Serve immediately and enjoy this cozy, soothing drink.

Nutritional Information: 50 calories, 1g protein, 5g carbohydrates, 3g fat, 1g fiber, 0mg cholesterol, 160mg sodium, 150mg potassium.

SUGAR-FREE HOT CHOCOLATE

Yield
2 servings

Preparation Time
5 minutes

Cooking Time
5 Minutes

INGREDIENTS

- 2 cups low-fat milk (or any milk of your choice)
- 2 tablespoons unsweetened cocoa powder
- 1-2 tablespoons maple syrup or a sugar-free sweetener (adjust to taste)
- 1/2 teaspoon vanilla extract
- A pinch of sea salt (optional, to enhance flavor)

DIRECTIONS

1. In a small saucepan, warm the milk over medium heat until it's hot but not boiling, stirring occasionally to prevent scorching.
2. Whisk in the cocoa powder until fully dissolved and smooth. Add the maple syrup or sugar-free sweetener and whisk until well combined.
3. Stir in the vanilla extract and a pinch of sea salt if using. Continue to heat for another minute, stirring continuously to ensure everything is well blended.
4. Pour the hot chocolate into two mugs and serve immediately. Enjoy this rich and satisfying drink as a guilt-free indulgence on cold days.

Nutritional Information: 100 calories, 6g protein, 14g carbohydrates, 3g fat, 2g fiber, 5mg cholesterol, 100mg sodium, 300mg potassium.

GOLDEN TURMERIC TEA

INGREDIENTS

- 2 cups water
- 1 teaspoon ground turmeric
- 1/2 teaspoon ground ginger (or 1 teaspoon freshly grated ginger)
- 1/2 teaspoon ground cinnamon (optional)
- 1 teaspoon maple syrup or a sugar-free sweetener (optional for added sweetness)
- 1/2 cup unsweetened almond milk (or any milk of your choice)
- A pinch of black pepper (to enhance the absorption of turmeric)

Yield
2 servings

Preparation Time
5 minutes

Cooking Time
10 Minutes

DIRECTIONS

1. Bring the water to a boil over medium heat in a small saucepan.
2. Once the water is boiling, reduce the heat to low and stir in the ground turmeric, ground ginger, and cinnamon if using. Simmer the mixture for about 5-7 minutes, stirring occasionally.
3. Remove the saucepan from the heat and strain the tea through a fine sieve into two cups to remove spice sediments.
4. Stir in the almond milk and add maple syrup or a sugar-free sweetener if desired. Add a pinch of black pepper to each cup to enhance the absorption of the turmeric.
5. Stir well and enjoy this warm, nourishing tea immediately.

Nutritional Information: 40 calories, 1g protein, 7g carbohydrates, 1.5g fat, 2g fiber, 0mg cholesterol, 180mg sodium, 150mg potassium.

GINGER LEMON HONEY TEA

Yield
2 servings

Preparation Time
5 minutes

Cooking Time
10 minutes

INGREDIENTS

- 2 cups water
- 1-inch piece of fresh ginger, peeled and thinly sliced
- 1 tablespoon lemon juice (about 1/2 lemon)
- 1-2 teaspoons honey or a sugar-free sweetener (adjust to taste)
- Lemon slices, for garnish (optional)

DIRECTIONS

1. Bring the water and ginger slices to a boil over medium heat in a small saucepan. Once boiling, reduce the heat and let it simmer for about 10 minutes to allow the ginger to infuse.
2. Remove the saucepan from the heat and strain the tea through a fine sieve into two cups to remove the ginger slices.
3. Stir in the lemon juice, honey, or sugar-free sweetener until fully dissolved. Adjust the sweetness to your taste.
4. Garnish with a lemon slice if desired and serve immediately. Enjoy this warm, soothing tea as a relaxing drink that's great for digestion.

Nutritional Information: 20 calories, 0g protein, 5g carbohydrates, 0g fat, 0g fiber, 0mg cholesterol, 10mg sodium, 60mg potassium.

SPICED CHAI LATTE

Yield
2 servings

Preparation Time
5 minutes

Cooking Time
10 Minutes

INGREDIENTS

- 2 cups water
- 2 black tea bags (or 2 teaspoons loose-leaf black tea)
- 1 cup unsweetened almond milk (or any milk of your choice)
- 1 cinnamon stick (or 1/2 teaspoon ground cinnamon)
- 4 whole cloves (or a pinch of ground cloves)
- 4 whole cardamom pods, slightly crushed (or 1/4 teaspoon ground cardamom)
- 1/2 teaspoon ground ginger (or a small piece of fresh ginger, sliced)
- 1 teaspoon maple syrup or a sugar-free sweetener (optional, adjust to taste)
- 1/2 teaspoon vanilla extract (optional)

DIRECTIONS

1. In a medium saucepan, bring the water to a boil. Add the cinnamon stick, cloves, cardamom, and ginger. Reduce the heat and let the spices simmer for 5 minutes to infuse the water with flavor.

2. Add the black tea bags to the simmering spiced water and steep for 3-5 minutes, depending on your preferred strength.

3. Remove the tea bags and stir in the almond milk. Add the maple syrup or sugar-free sweetener if used, and heat the mixture gently until warm. Stir in the vanilla extract if desired.

4. Pour the spiced chai latte into two mugs, straining the spices if necessary. Serve immediately and enjoy this warm, aromatic drink.

Nutritional Information: 50 calories, 1g protein, 9g carbohydrates, 2g fat, 1g fiber, 0mg cholesterol, 50mg sodium, 100mg potassium.

FRUIT AND VEGGIE JUICES

CARROT APPLE GINGER JUICE

Yield
2 servings

Preparation Time
10 minutes

Cooking Time
0 Minutes

INGREDIENTS

- 4 medium carrots, peeled and chopped
- 2 medium apples, cored and chopped
- 1-inch piece of fresh ginger, peeled
- 1/2 lemon, juiced (optional for added brightness)

DIRECTIONS

1. Peel and chop the carrots, core and chop the apples, and peel the ginger.
2. Process the carrots, apples, and ginger until smooth using a juicer. If you don't have a juicer, blend the ingredients in a high-powered blender with a little water, then strain through a fine mesh sieve or cheesecloth to remove the pulp.
3. If desired, stir in the juice of half a lemon for added brightness and flavor.
4. Pour the juice into two glasses and serve immediately. Enjoy this vibrant, nutrient-packed drink as a refreshing and energizing start to your day.

Nutritional Information: 120 calories, 1g protein, 30g carbohydrates, 0g fat, 5g fiber, 0mg cholesterol, 30mg sodium, 450mg potassium.

BEET AND BERRY BOOST JUICE

Yield
2 servings

Preparation Time
10 minutes

Cooking Time
0 Minutes

INGREDIENTS

- 1 medium beet, peeled and chopped
- 1/2 cup mixed berries (fresh or frozen)
- 1/2 cup fresh orange juice (from about 1-2 oranges)
- 1/4 cup cold water (optional, for blending if using a blender)

DIRECTIONS

1. Peel and chop the beet. If using fresh berries, rinse them thoroughly.
2. Using a juicer, process the beet and mixed berries until smooth. If you don't have a juicer, blend the ingredients in a high-powered blender with the cold water until smooth, then strain through a fine mesh sieve or cheesecloth to remove the pulp.
3. Stir in the fresh orange juice to add sweetness and enhance the flavor.
4. Pour the juice into two glasses and serve immediately. Enjoy this vibrant, antioxidant-rich drink that's both sweet and earthy.

Nutritional Information: 110 calories, 2g protein, 27g carbohydrates, 0g fat, 4g fiber, 0mg cholesterol, 20mg sodium, 400mg potassium.

GREEN DETOX JUICE

Yield
2 servings

Preparation Time
10 minutes

Cooking Time
0 Minutes

INGREDIENTS

- 2 cups fresh spinach leaves
- 1/2 cucumber, peeled and chopped
- 1 green apple, cored and chopped
- 1/2 lemon, juiced
- 1/2 cup cold water (optional for blending if using a blender)

DIRECTIONS

1. Rinse the spinach leaves, peel and chop the cucumber, and core and chop the green apple.
2. Using a juicer, process the spinach, cucumber, and green apple until smooth. If you don't have a juicer, blend the ingredients in a high-powered blender with the cold water until smooth, then strain through a fine mesh sieve or cheesecloth to remove the pulp.
3. Stir in the juice of half a lemon to enhance the flavor and boost the detoxifying effects.
4. Pour the juice into two glasses and serve immediately. Enjoy this refreshing and detoxifying drink packed with vitamins and minerals.

Nutritional Information: 80 calories, 1g protein, 20g carbohydrates, 0g fat, 3g fiber, 0mg cholesterol, 15mg sodium, 350mg potassium.

CITRUS CARROT COOLER

Yield
2 servings

Preparation Time
10 minutes

Cooking Time
0 minutes

INGREDIENTS

- 4 medium carrots, peeled and chopped
- 1 cup freshly squeezed orange juice (from about 2-3 oranges)
- 1/2 lime, juiced
- 1/4 cup cold water (optional for blending if using a blender)
- Ice cubes (optional for serving)

DIRECTIONS

1. Peel and chop the carrots. Squeeze the juice from the oranges and lime.
2. Process the carrots until smooth using a juicer. If you don't have a juicer, blend the carrots in a high-powered blender with the cold water until smooth, then strain through a fine mesh sieve or cheesecloth to remove the pulp.
3. Combine the freshly squeezed orange, lime, and carrot juice in a large pitcher. Stir well to blend the flavors.
4. Pour the juice into two glasses over ice cubes if desired. Serve immediately and enjoy this refreshing, immune-boosting drink.

Nutritional Information: 110 calories, 2g protein, 27g carbohydrates, 0g fat, 3g fiber, 0mg cholesterol, 30mg sodium, 450mg potassium.

APPLE KALE POWER JUICE

Yield

2 servings

Preparation Time

10 minutes

Cooking Time

0 Minutes

INGREDIENTS

- 2 cups fresh kale leaves, washed and stems removed
- 2 medium apples, cored and chopped
- 1/2 lemon, juiced
- 1/2 cup cold water (optional for blending if using a blender)

DIRECTIONS

1. Rinse the kale leaves thoroughly and remove the stems. Core and chop the apples.

2. Using a juicer, process the kale leaves and apples until smooth. If you don't have a juicer, blend the ingredients in a high-powered blender with the cold water until smooth, then strain through a fine mesh sieve or cheesecloth to remove the pulp.

3. Stir in the juice of half a lemon to enhance the flavor and add a zesty brightness.

4. Pour the juice into two glasses and serve immediately. This nutrient-dense and refreshing drink is a powerful way to fuel your day.

Nutritional Information: 90 calories, 1g protein, 23g carbohydrates, 0g fat, 4g fiber, 0mg cholesterol, 20mg sodium, 350mg potassium.

CHAPTER 9

DINING OUT AND SOCIAL EVENTS

EATING OUT STRATEGIES

Eating out doesn't have to mean giving up on your healthy eating goals. With a few smart strategies, you can enjoy dining out without worrying about your blood sugar.

- **Plan Ahead:** If possible, check the restaurant's menu online before you go. Look for dishes that are grilled, baked, or steamed rather than fried. Many places also offer low-carb or diabetic-friendly options.

- **Control Portions:** Restaurants tend to serve large portions. Don't hesitate to ask for a to-go box right away and save half for later. This way, you can manage portion sizes and avoid overeating.

- **Watch Out for Hidden Sugars:** Dressings, sauces, and even some soups can be loaded with sugar. Opt for olive oil and vinegar for salads, ask for sauces on the side, and choose dishes that are made fresh rather than heavily processed.

- **Prioritize Protein and Veggies:** Focus on meals that emphasize lean proteins like chicken, fish, or tofu, and pair them with plenty of non-starchy veggies. Skip the bread basket or ask for whole-grain alternatives if available.

NAVIGATING SOCIAL EVENTS

Parties, holidays, and social events can be tricky when you're managing diabetes, but with some planning, you can still enjoy the occasion while sticking to your diet.

- **Eat Before You Go:** Don't arrive at a party starving. Have a small snack with protein and fiber beforehand to curb your hunger and prevent overeating.

- **Bring Your Own Dish:** If it's a potluck or gathering, offer to bring a diabetic-friendly dish. That way, you know there will be something healthy to enjoy, and others may appreciate it too!

- **Be Mindful of Drinks:** Watch out for sugary drinks and cocktails. Opt for water, sparkling water, or diet sodas. If you do drink alcohol, limit it and have it with food to help manage your blood sugar.

- **Practice Portion Control:** Social events can often mean indulgent food. Take small portions of what you want to try and fill up on vegetables and lean proteins.

Dining out and attending social events can be enjoyable while following a diabetic diet. A little planning and mindful choices can go a long way!

CHAPTER 10

MEAL PLANNING

MEAL PLANNING TIPS FOR DIABETICS

Meal planning can be one of the best tools for managing diabetes. It helps you stay on track with your diet, saves you time during the week, and takes the guesswork out of what to eat. Plus, when you plan, you're more likely to make healthy choices that steady your blood sugar levels. Let's dive into some simple and friendly tips to help you start with meal planning.

1 Start with a Balanced Plate

A great way to plan your meals is to use the "balanced plate" method. Here's how it works:

Half your plate should contain non-starchy vegetables like leafy greens, broccoli, bell peppers, or cauliflower. These are low in carbs and high in nutrients.

A quarter of your plate should be lean protein, such as chicken, fish, tofu, or legumes. Protein helps keep you full and supports stable blood sugar levels.

The remaining quarter is for healthy carbohydrates like whole grains, starchy vegetables (like sweet potatoes), or fruit. These carbs are slower to digest, which helps prevent spikes in blood sugar.

2 Plan for Consistent Meals and Snacks

Eating at regular intervals can help keep your blood sugar levels steady throughout the day. Aim to have three balanced meals and one or two snacks at roughly the exact times each day. Planning your meals ensures that you have the proper foods on hand and can help you avoid reaching for less healthy options when you're hungry.

3 Focus on Whole Foods

When planning your meals, include as many whole foods as possible. Fresh fruits and vegetables, whole grains, lean proteins, and healthy fats are the foundation of a good meal plan. These foods are nutrient-dense, filling, and less likely to cause spikes in blood sugar.

4 Include a Variety of Foods

Variety is the spice of life — and it's also vital to a healthy diet. Including a wide range of foods in your meal plan keeps things interesting and ensures you get all the nutrients your body needs. Try to mix up your protein sources, rotate through different vegetables, and experiment with new whole grains to keep your meals exciting.

5 Prep Ahead for the Week

Meal prepping can save you a ton of time during the week and help you stick to your meal plan. Spend a little time on the weekend or whenever you have free time to prepare some meals in advance. You can chop veggies, cook grains, grill chicken, or make a big batch of soup to portion out for the week. Having healthy, ready-to-eat meals on hand makes it easier to avoid less healthy convenience foods.

6 Be Mindful of Portions

Portion control is important when managing diabetes, especially with carbohydrates. Using measuring cups, a food scale, or the plate method mentioned earlier can help you keep portions in check. Remember, even healthy foods can affect your blood sugar if you eat too much of them, so it's all about finding the right balance.

7 Don't Forget to Hydrate

Water is an essential part of any healthy diet. Drinking enough water throughout the day helps keep your body functioning properly and can even help regulate your blood sugar levels. When planning your meals, think about incorporating hydrating foods like cucumbers, tomatoes, and leafy greens, and make sure to drink plenty of water with your meals.

8 Allow Flexibility and Enjoyment

Meal planning doesn't have to be rigid. It's okay to swap out meals or adjust your plan as needed. The goal is to create a structure that supports your health while also being enjoyable and sustainable. Don't forget to include some of your favorite foods and allow yourself to enjoy treats in moderation—diabetes management is about balance, not deprivation.

9 Plan for Dining Out

Eating out doesn't have to derail your meal plan. Look at restaurant menus in advance if possible and choose dishes that fit into your plan—think grilled meats, steamed veggies, and whole grains. Don't be afraid to ask for modifications like dressing on the side or substituting extra vegetables for starchy sides.

10   Keep Track and Adjust

As you plan and prepare your meals, keep track of what works well for you and what doesn't. Everyone's body responds differently to different foods, so finding what works best for you might take a little time. Don't be afraid to adjust your plan based on how you're feeling and your blood sugar levels are responding.

HOW TO CREATE YOUR MEAL PLAN?

Meal planning might seem like a lot of work at first, but once you get the hang of it, it becomes second nature. Your effort in planning your meals pays off in better blood sugar control, more energy, and a greater sense of well-being. Plus, it makes eating healthy, delicious meals something you can look forward to daily.

So grab a notebook, pick a few recipes from this cookbook, and plan your weekly meals.

Here's a step-by-step guide to help you create a practical and easy-to-follow meal plan:

1   Determine Nutritional Goals

- **Calorie Intake:** Estimate daily calorie needs based on age, gender, activity level, and weight management goals. Use online calculators or consult a dietitian for precision.
- **Macronutrient Distribution:** For a diabetic meal plan, focus on:
  - o **Carbohydrates:** Limit to about 45-60 grams per meal, depending on individual needs.
  - o **Proteins:** Include lean sources like fish, chicken, or plant-based proteins.
  - o **Fats:** Emphasize healthy fats (e.g., olive oil, avocado) while reducing saturated fats.

2   Select Diabetes-Friendly Foods

Focus on low-carb, low-sugar, and nutrient-dense options:

- **Vegetables:** Leafy greens, broccoli, peppers, cucumbers, etc.
- **Fruits:** Berries, apples (in moderation), and citrus.
- **Whole Grains:** Quinoa, barley, whole oats.
- **Lean Proteins:** Chicken, turkey, tofu, fish.
- **Healthy Fats:** Nuts, seeds, olive oil, avocado.
- **Dairy Alternatives:** Unsweetened almond or coconut milk.

3   Structure the Plan by Meals

For a balanced diabetic diet, include three main meals (breakfast, lunch, dinner) and 1-2 snacks. Here's an example structure.

Breakfast:

- Scrambled eggs with spinach and mushrooms (Protein + Veggies)
- 1 slice of whole-grain toast (Carb)
- A handful of mixed berries (Fruit)

Mid-Morning Snack:

- A small apple (Fruit)
- 1 tablespoon peanut butter (Healthy Fat)

Lunch:

- Grilled chicken salad with mixed greens, tomatoes, cucumbers, olive oil, and vinegar (Protein + Veggies + Healthy Fat)
- ½ cup of quinoa (Carb)

Afternoon Snack:

- Greek yogurt (Protein)
- A few almonds (Healthy Fat)

Dinner:

- Baked salmon with a lemon-dill sauce (Protein)
- Roasted broccoli and carrots (Veggies)
- Cauliflower rice (Low-carb option)

Evening Snack (optional):

- A small handful of walnuts (Healthy Fat)
- Slices of cucumber or celery sticks (Veggies)

4 Incorporate Variety

Rotate proteins, vegetables, and grains throughout the week to keep the meal plan interesting and prevent burnout. Aim for different cooking methods (grilling, roasting, steaming) and flavors.

5 Balance and Portion Control

- **Use the Plate Method:** For each meal, fill half the plate with non-starchy vegetables, a quarter with lean proteins, and a quarter with whole grains or starchy vegetables.
- **Measure Portions:** Use tools like measuring cups and scales to ensure portions are in line with the diabetic dietary needs.

6 Plan for the Week

Prepare a meal schedule for 7 days, ensuring balanced nutrition each day. Here's an outline:

Meal	Monday	Tuesday	Wednesday	Thursday	Friday	Saturday	Sunday
Breakfast	Scrambled eggs + whole wheat toast	Greek yogurt + berries	Oatmeal + walnuts	Almond flour pancakes + strawberries	Avocado toast + boiled egg	Chia seed pudding + almonds	Veggie omelette + cottage cheese
Snack 1	Apple + peanut butter	Cucumber slices + hummus	Handful of almonds	Celery sticks + almond butter	Carrot sticks + guacamole	Mixed nuts	Cherry tomatoes + mozzarella
Lunch	Grilled chicken salad + olive oil	Turkey wrap + veggies	Quinoa + veggie stir-fry	Chicken + arugula power bowl	Tuna& spinach salad	Mediterranean chickpea bowl	Baked salmon + steamed broccoli
Snack 2	Celery sticks + cream cheese	Small orange + cottage cheese	Greek yogurt + chia seeds	Cottage cheese + berries	Bell pepper slices + hummus	Pear + cheddar slices	Handful of sunflower seeds
Dinner	Baked salmon + roasted Brussels sprouts	Chicken breast + quinoa	Tofu stir-fry + brown rice	Turkey meatloaf + roasted veggies	Grilled shrimp + cauliflower rice	Baked chicken + asparagus	Eggplant + cauliflower curry

Include a Shopping List

Based on your meal plan, prepare a shopping list with all the necessary ingredients, ensuring you have everything needed for the week.

7 Adapt for Special Diets or Preferences

Customize the plan based on individual needs like vegetarian, vegan, gluten-free, or specific calorie requirements. For example, substitute animal proteins with plant-based options like beans or tofu.

8 Prep in Advance

- **Batch Cooking:** Prepare some meals or key ingredients (e.g., grilled chicken, roasted veggies) in bulk and store them for easy access during the week.

- **Meal Prep Containers:** Store meals ahead of time in portion-sized containers, ensuring that each meal adheres to the dietary goals.

9 Monitor and Adjust

Regularly check how the plan works for blood sugar management, satiety, and energy levels. Adjust portion sizes, food choices, or meal timing to suit personal health goals better.

By following these steps, you can create a diabetic meal plan that is nutritious, easy to follow, and tailored to individual health needs and preferences.

CONCLUSION

As you've explored this cookbook, you've taken an essential step toward better health. Managing diabetes doesn't mean sacrificing flavor or enjoyment in your meals. It's about finding balance, making mindful choices, and embracing a healthier lifestyle that allows you to enjoy delicious food.

Remember, the journey to better health is not about perfection but progress. Celebrate each step, whether mastering a new recipe, planning your meals, or making healthier choices when dining out. These small, consistent efforts can lead to significant changes over time.

You have the power to take control of your health, and it starts with the choices you make every day. With the right tools and a positive mindset, managing diabetes can become a natural part of your life. Keep experimenting in the kitchen, have fun with your meals, and don't hesitate to get creative!

Here's to your health, happiness, and a future filled with nourishing, delicious food.

INDEX

Made in the USA
Monee, IL
10 March 2025

13790326R00066